UNDERSTANDING
& INVESTIGATING
ART

LERY into the Art Room

UNDERSTANDING & INVESTIGATING ART

Bringing the NATIONAL GALLERY into the Art Room

ROD TAYLOR

In association with
National Gallery Publications

Hodder & Stoughton
A MEMBER OF THE HODDER HEADLINE GROUP

Order queries: please contact Bookpoint Ltd, 130 Milton Park, Abingdon, Oxon OX14 4SB.
Telephone: (44) 01235 827720, Fax: (44) 01235 400454. Lines are open from 9.00–6.00,
Monday to Saturday, with a 24 hour message answering service.

You can also order through our website www.hodderheadline.co.uk

British Library Cataloguing in Publication Data
A catalogue record for this title is available from The British Library

ISBN 0340 67989 1

First published 1999
Impression number   10   9   8   7   6   5
Year   2006   2005   2004   2003

Typeset by Wearset, Boldon, Tyne and Wear
Printed in China for Hodder & Stoughton Educational, a division of Hodder Headline
Ltd 338 Euston Road, London NW1 3BH by Colorcraft Ltd.

CONTENTS

Acknowledgements

Many people have contributed in countless ways to *Understanding & Investigating Art*. Special thanks are due to Neil MacGregor, the Director of the National Gallery, and all the gallery staff who have helped in so many ways. In particular, I must thank Patricia Williams, Director of Publications at the National Gallery. The concept of a book linking National Curriculum requirements to the National Gallery collection arose directly out of discussions with her. Involved from the outset, she then used all her professional skills and acumen to help nurture the project. In the process, she lifted many seemingly insurmountable burdens off my shoulders. Special thanks are also due to Erika Langmuir. Her highly informative *National Gallery Companion Guide* was, indeed, my constant companion throughout. In addition, though, she read the manuscript at a draft stage, promptly returning each chapter with comments and observations that were always sympathetic, apt and full of insight. I have benefited enormously from her profound and detailed knowledge of the National Gallery collection and her willingness to openly share this.

I must also thank Catherine Boulton, Commissioning Editor at Hodder and Stoughton, for her commitment to the project.

Thanks are also due to Nigel Leighton, Drumcroon's Head of Centre in Wigan, for his energy in involving teachers in the project and acquiring funding to enable considerable numbers of Y9 Wigan students to work in north-western and London galleries in ways relevant to the project. The *Universal Themes* exhibition he organised at Drumcroon in 1996 marked another important link between project principles and student practice. I would also like to thank all the Wigan teachers involved, especially Pauline Wood, Head of Art at Leigh Bedford High School for the related ways in which her Y8 students made use of the 1996 Sainsbury's reproductions for schools. The brief outline of this initiative in the Introduction illustrates the transferable nature of the principles, and highlights how beneficial they are to any school that uses them systematically.

The author and publishers would like to thank the following for help in producing this book:

Patricia Williams and Jan Green at National Gallery Publications, Dr Erika Langmuir, Eve Poland at The British Museum.

Designed by Lynda King.

Project Editor: Eleanor Stillwell.

Desk Editor: Alexia Clifford.

Understanding & Investigating Art: the Audience

Understanding and Investigating Art is for use by teachers and students of secondary school age in art studio, gallery and environmental contexts. Teachers will find it helpful in their lesson planning and in constructing a whole-school curriculum that takes positive account of continuity, progression and coherence. This book highlights a range of approaches that are designed to extend, enrich and reanimate what is on offer within any school syllabus. It also explores a set of principles and working methods that are relevant to all phases of education. It can be used with groups of students, or teachers can direct individual students to specific activities that relate to their personal strengths and interests, or particular weaknesses or omissions in their work. Individual students can make informed use of the book by working on their own to supplement and extend their school work. Or they can use it to cultivate and pursue personal interests in greater depth with regard to their practical work, critical studies issues, gallery visits, and the study of their locality.

National Curriculum Art Requirements

The book addresses many National Curriculum Art requirements. The most innovative feature of the National Curriculum is probably its stipulation that students' 'understanding and enjoyment of art, craft and design should be developed through activities that bring together requirements from both **Investigating and Making** and **Knowledge and Understanding**, wherever possible.' In order to develop their appreciation of our diverse cultural heritage, students 'should be introduced to the work of artists, craftspeople and designers'. The selection should include work in a variety of genres and styles from the locality, the past and present, and a variety of cultures, Western and non-Western. The Western tradition 'should be exemplified by works chosen from the Classical and Medieval, Renaissance and post-Renaissance periods through to the twentieth century'. Works selected from non-Western cultures 'should exemplify a range of traditions from different times and places'.

Students should also be taught to 'develop understanding of the work of artists, craftspeople and designers, applying this to their own work'. GCSE examinations have been modified to take account of these requirements and, at the time of writing the ways in which A levels can be similarly modified are under consideration. For the first time, therefore, all students now have a right to an education that makes them knowledgeable and informed about art and artists in ways that directly connect with their own art practice. When the approach is genuinely interactive, each aspect has the potential to mutually enrich and affirm the other. In the process, students become active participants in the culture, as opposed to being passive recipients of it. A wide range of critical studies strategies and approaches have influenced practice in many schools in recent years. In order to properly address their students' entitlement needs, it is necessary for all schools to systematically adopt these on an ongoing basis.

The Historical Legacy

In practice, though, the National Curriculum requirements are complex. Many recently-graduated PGCE students report that they still receive an art college training that keeps theory and practice apart. Art theory and practice have long been treated separately in schools, and this approach still strongly shapes and influences many teachers' attitudes. A chronological treatment of art history and appreciation filtered down into schools at the A level phase, but any links with students' practical work were often purely coincidental or accidental. This kind of approach to art history was generally deemed to be inappropriate with younger students so, by default, little tuition about art and artists took place. This problem was further compounded by the widely-held belief that students' originality and creativity is impaired once they are subject to adult influences. As a consequence, most courses prior to A level were purely practical, meaning the vast majority of students left school knowing little or nothing about art in any wider sense.

Janet, a primary school teacher of 17 years' experience, vividly highlights the nature of these problems. She recently returned to college to study Foundation Art & Design with the intention of rectifying these omissions in her own education. She cannot recall ever being shown any artists' work before starting A levels. Once she did, the 'impact of art history lectures and my first encounters with the great art of Masaccio, Caravaggio, Rembrandt and Vermeer was enormous'. Unfortunately, she had no opportunity 'to make connections between the great (and what I saw as inaccessible) art masters, and what I was experiencing in my own practice. A student's excited discoveries could not be enacted, thus elements such as composition, *chiaroscuro* and foreshortening lay untried, leaving me unchallenged practically.'

Deprived for years, she became quite a privileged student during the A level stage, for she clearly derived great enjoyment and benefit from her art history lectures. On the other hand, though, without teacher help and support, she was unable to make use of the qualities she admired in other artists' work, to the disadvantage of her own practice. On continuing her studies in higher education, she encountered an even worse situation: 'Amazingly, throughout a four-year degree course, I never saw another artist's sketchbook or preparatory work, or had the experience of using and keeping one myself'.

This leads her to consider the dictum that 'Art grows out of art', and to 'examine the extent to which an individual can assimilate and translate aesthetic experience in order to re-invent forms and establish new ways of seeing and responding'. She now fully appreciates the importance of introducing even the youngest children she teaches to a wide range and variety of art works, to help them make connections between these and their own work. Thematic approaches are invaluable to this process, and make it possible to bring together the requirements of both **Investigating and Making** and **Knowledge and Understanding**.

The Format of 'Understanding & Investigating Art'

With this in mind, *Understanding & Investigating Art* uses 'Universal Themes' as a basis. Each chapter provides an in-depth insight into each of the following:

The Human Figure: identity and relationships
Environments: natural and made
Flora & Fauna
Events: personal, communal and historical
The Fantastic & Strange: myth, metamorphosis and dream
The Abstract: form and meaning

These themes are sufficiently wide and generous in scope to group together all the works in any gallery or museum collection, with inevitable overlaps, of course! The topics comprising the school art curriculum can also be grouped together under these themes. Through contextualisation, it is therefore possible to make connections all the time between art and artists, and what the students are doing in their own practice. In this text, therefore, a natural ebb and flow exists between the study of works of art in the gallery, museum and locality, and a range of possible practical activities students might undertake in relation to them. The approach consciously seeks to bring together the requirements of **Investigating and Making** and **Knowledge and Understanding**.

Paintings in the National Gallery provide the main focus of the text, and are used to exemplify major aspects of the Western tradition. Examples are drawn from the different European nationalities and periods, ranging from the medieval to the 20th century. A small number of works from the British Museum 'exemplify a range of traditions from different times and places', and provide a glimpse of how the themes manifest themselves in the art of the other four continents of the world. My own photographs of architecture, sculpture, monuments and signs in public places are used to represent the art of the locality. These range from examples to do with civic pride, or commemorating major events, to pub signs. As such, they embrace popular forms of culture as well as what is often termed 'high art' examples.

Exploring Thematic Approaches

Each theme is worthy of in-depth study, for it has the potential to shape and influence artists' work in significant ways. Kaffe Fassett, a textile artist, provides a fascinating insight into why the flora aspects of 'Flora & Fauna' are so vital to his work. 'This most joyously universal of themes seems to bring a musical lightness to whatever it graces'. Flowers are 'a constantly renewing theme. In knitting I usually treat them in a stylised, flat manner, whereas I use a more realistic and detailed approach in my needlepoint.' Their magic in decorations is 'eternal', as can be seen in the arts and crafts of all cultures. 'The frail, ephemeral quality of a flower amazes me again and again, especially after studying the decorative portraits of them painted on furniture and porcelain, woven and embroidered on fabrics and carved on stone.' The fruits and vegetables 'born of flowers' is another related and recurring theme in decorations, and he is enthralled by Dutch, Italian, Turkish and Oriental paintings of fruits and vegetables. 'I have found good sources of these subjects on dishes, box labels, wrapping paper and reproductions of old still lifes.

He is always on the look out for fresh examples, and surrounds himself with them in his studio. Glancing up from his work to the studio pinboard, the cards and cuttings that catch his eye include, 'a rose on a scrap of linoleum found in a skip, fat Victorian roses decorating a sewing accessories packet, embroidered flowers from Yugoslavia, stylised painted flowers on a Chinese burial paper, and rows of tulips from a Turkish embroidery, knitted as a swatch for a new jacket. There is a lattice of 18th century flowers from a chair back and a delicate painting of Japanese flowers. All these different flower moods, styles and colourings are just a taste of possibilities to be found, collected and then revitalised by the knitter and needlepointer'.

He recalls 'one amazing day' from his youth. A friend took him to the Victoria and Albert Museum, where he discovered under one roof, 'carpets, embroideries, jewelled boxes, Indian miniatures, costumes and fans of many ages, highly decorated musical instruments and, most exciting of all to my eye, room after room of beautifully patterned china'. He returned again and again, spending hours alone 'sketching bits of mosaic, china pots, textiles – anything with a pattern became grist to my mill. I ate, slept and drank patterns, and the V&A was one large storehouse of them'. He makes use of this stimulus to this day. 'Working from sources in the V&A is a gift to a textile designer. From old embroideries to the wonderfully painted china, there are plenty of examples of strong, simple shapes of fruits and vegetables in interesting colours. Often I just take the shape and add my own colour'.

He highlights a number of basic critical studies principles. He is knowledgeable about and enjoys flora in art for its own sake, and this has developed into a lifelong passion. Seeing and studying examples in the original was crucial to his development, emphasising how important gallery and museum visits are to any balanced art education. In his own work, he draws so freely on his art history interests that his knowledge and enjoyment of flora in art has almost become inseparable from his working methods and approaches and, indeed, his own work. He collects and surrounds himself with all kinds of relevant examples, displaying them in his studio where he can easily see them while he works. This form of studio contextualisation enables him to group together examples drawn from different times, places and cultures, according to his needs. It also reflects a basic human urge to collect, group and arrange, and surround ourselves with the things about which we feel passionate.

These procedures, and the in-depth exploration of one theme, are not only relevant to mature artists. Students of school age can benefit enormously from them, too. Stuart finds his greatest motivation in environments. In a written A level Personal Appraisal statement, he reveals how long-term his interest is, and what a profound impact a gallery exhibition had on him as a GCSE student.

> 'My art work has improved a lot from my knowledge of other art works and history. It has given me lots of ideas, in content, theme and subject matter. In the artists I have researched, their colour values and processes have influenced me a great deal also. I have been very interested because my subject matter is landscapes and I like to use oil paint as my material, and the artists I have researched use these. Since I was young I have enjoyed drawing and painting landscapes, but when I saw Ian Murphy's *Landmarks* exhibition at Drumcroon when I was at school, it got me hooked on oils and I began to experiment using lots of texture

on my canvas, creating an impasto effect, very similar to Murphy's. When I researched the artists Constable and Turner, it brought new ideas and processes into my work. I prefer to work outside, here I mainly do sketches which I work from to produce finished pieces. I am very interested in mood and atmosphere and how light affects this, which has great connections in my research.'

The impact of the *Landmarks* exhibition has continued to influence his researches into other artists' work and his own practice. His interest in landscape was powerfully reflected in his GCSE exhibition, and continued to motivate him throughout his A level course. In his written Personal Study on 'Light, Mood and Atmosphere', he addressed continuity and change in art by connecting Constable and Turner's treatment of the elements with Murphy's. He was able to interview Murphy, a young local artist, as an essential part of his research. His passion for landscape sustained him throughout his Foundation Art & Design course, and his explorations into this aspect of the Universal Theme of Environments continue to inform his degree-level Fine Art studies to this day.

Curriculum Breadth and Balance

Many artists choose to devote themselves to the field of study they find most significant to them. Ideally, though, their chosen area of specialisation will arise out of a full awareness of the range of options and possibilities that are open to them, as opposed to what they feel secure with, born of ignorance. Leonardo considered that the painter who is not universal 'is not worthy of praise', and to qualify as 'universal' must possess wide-ranging skills. It is a poor artist, he maintained, who:

> '. . . makes only a single figure well. For do you not see how many and varied are the actions performed by men alone? Do you not see how many different animals there are, and also trees and plants and flowers? What variety of mountainous regions and plains, of springs, rivers and cities with public buildings, instruments fitted for man's use; of diverse costumes, ornaments and arts? All these things should be rendered with equal facility and perfection by whomever you wish to call a good painter.'

The concept of 'universal artist' is not embraced much today. Expertise within a narrow specialist field is increasingly sought and highly regarded. However, in order to recognise where their real interests and aptitudes lie, it is important that all students – certainly up to and including the Key Stage 3 level – receive a sufficiently broad and balanced art education to provide a basis for them to make informed choices. As an essential part of this, students should address and revisit each Universal Theme regularly to carry out their investigating and making activities, and to increase their knowledge and understanding of art and artists.

Some of these themes are more neglected than others at present. A disturbing number of young people testify to never dealing with the human figure while at school, for instance. Therefore, it is reasonable for a school to analyse the opportunities it currently provides for the study of each Universal Theme. What activities relate to the human figure, for example? Do these involve *all* students, or are they optional? When, where, how and why do activities related to this theme occur?

How regularly is it revisited? Does any undue repetition occur? Do projects adequately take account of, and build upon preceding ones? Are the activities sufficiently varied, and do they provide a challenging and rigorous course on the human figure? What scope is there for improving the activities on offer?

A curriculum audit, looking at each theme in this way, provides an overview of the place each theme currently occupies in the curriculum, and whether some are unduly neglected or not revisited on a regular basis. In order to deal with each one in sufficient depth, and to encompass an adequate range of attainment target requirements each project should be of several weeks' duration. Treating each theme for an average period of about half a term, enables each one to be revisited on an annual basis. Longer timespans can obviously also be achieved by periodically grouping two or more themes together.

A Thematic Case Study

The topic 'Victor and Vanquished' enabled Year 8 students in a Wigan high school to confront a wide range of major life and death issues. It was used to establish links between a painting of a great human drama, *The Triumph of David* by Poussin, and one of conflict in the animal kingdom, *Cheetah and Stag with Two Indians* by Stubbs, two of the Sainsbury's 1996 reproductions for schools. The schools' art curriculum is structured around Universal Themes, so the topic was chosen in the full knowledge the students would be dealing with two Universal Themes: the Human Figure and the fauna aspect of Flora & Fauna.

Marjan Wouda (see page 70), an artist already known to some students through her work in the Artists in Wigan Schools Scheme, was in residence during the project. Her *Chanticleer* sculptures of foxes and cockerels address issues to do with victor and vanquished from both animal and human perspectives, making her an ideal choice. Her sculptures were on display in the art room in close proximity to a stuffed fox and cockerel, and animal skeletons and skulls. Her drawn studies and animal maquettes were also on display in her studio space, alongside Stubbs' anatomical drawings and Muybridge's 'Animal Locomotion' photographs. With the artist and teacher working in partnership, the students made studies of a cat, owned by the head of department, and of their peers in poses designed to emulate the body language of animals, either as hunter or hunted. This work was further substantiated by their homework sketchbook studies of pets, full of body language.

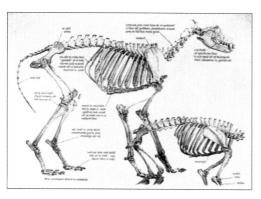

The framed Poussin and Stubbs reproductions were centrally hung on one wall. Images of sculptures of David illustrated the status the subject enjoyed in the Renaissance and during Poussin's lifetime. A sculpture of Boudicea and Rodin's *The Burghers of Calais* (see page 109) showed the contrast in body language between victor and vanquished. Gothic carvings raised issues of role reversal. Is the vanquished actually the victor once the status of sainthood or martyrdom is conferred? The Stubbs raised similar kinds of issues with regard to the animal kingdom.

All the material was captioned, and included questions as well as imparting information. Through these, students were able to broaden their awareness of the topic in art, and began to formulate their own ideas. They drew comparisons between the stiff nature of the Gothic carvings, the harmonious relationships apparent in the Renaissance art of Donatello and Michelangelo, and the more obviously dynamic twisting Baroque rhythms favoured by Bernini. Postcards and bookplates provided further evidence of the treatment of the topic in art through time, and across place and cultures. In addition, the teacher related the topic to the students and everyday life by introducing it through newspaper headlines of topical sporting events and items on stalking, bullying, local disputes, war and strife.

Students were allowed a generous amount of time to analyse and respond to the Poussin and Stubbs paintings during one session. They made notes while discussing the paintings in small groups of three or four. To aid their discussions, they had question papers in which a wide range of issues about the content, form, process and mood of the works were posed. Under 'content', they unravelled the drama of the celebrations following David's victory over Goliath, but once they focused on form, they began talking in terms of pure geometry about the triangles and squares the painting was composed of. Under 'process', they worked out they were both oil paintings. On actually seeing the Stubbs in Manchester City Art Gallery, though, they were immediately responsive to areas of thick and thin paint, the use of translucent paint to render transparent fabrics, and the texture of fur – especially the wispy bits under the cheetah's stomach! Standing in front of it, the powerful mood it exerted after this period of study made an enormous impact on them.

Students worked in clay with Marjan, constructing animal heads or half-relief sculptures of animals as predators or the hunted. They used their own drawings of animals made from life, but their attention was constantly being drawn to the bones and skeletons on display, the anatomical studies of Stubbs, and other resource material. They focused on the anatomical structure of each animal, starting by constructing clay ribs and bones, and then adding layer on layer, finally arriving at the outer surface, appearance and posture of the animal. Another group worked from students posed in football kit or as supporters, some as winners, others as losers. Using pastel, paint, collage and resist techniques, they produced large-scale paintings. A third group also worked in clay, building models of heads and shoulders from their own design sheets. Some developed the role-reversal idea humorously – a mouse catching a man, for example. They were taught specific constructional skills, for some had no previous experience of using clay. Skills were not acquired by teaching the elements of art in isolation, though, but in relation to students' ideas, rich in content and meaning, and through constant reference to the work of other artists, showing how they had dealt with similar problems.

This project unmistakably brings together a wide range of 'requirements from both **Investigating and Making** and **Knowledge and Understanding**'. Similar principles and approaches underpin every other project undertaken by Year 8, who in the course of the year, cover all the Universal Themes, as do students in year 7 and 9. Each theme highlights specific criteria for assessment, establishing consistency between the end-of-key-stage profile and end-of-Year 7 and 8 assessments. Staff, students and parents can therefore monitor any student's progress right through a key stage using sets of criteria that have a clarity and consistency often absent from student assessment in art.

Making Gallery Links and Connections

While in the gallery, the students' brief also required them to locate other works with relevance to their theme, and to analyse and respond to them by posing similar questions. Neil MacGregor, Director of the National Gallery, says the gallery 'is not just a collection of great pictures, it is also a collection of hundreds of different worlds', and the same is true of most art gallery collections. Instead of trying to see everything and wandering aimlessly about, it is far better that students enter into just four or so of these worlds on one gallery visit. Had the students been exploring 'Victor and Vanquished' in the National Gallery, their three extra works could easily follow the opening sequence of the Fantastic & Strange chapter. Two followers of Cadmus are being devoured by a dragon, two versions of St George defeating the dragon are compared, Ulysses is deriding Polyphemus, Apollo is killing the Cyclops, and Phineas and his followers are being turned to stone by Perseus. These examples alone span four centuries, and include artists from Holland, Italy, France and Britain. The book helps students make the most of gallery visits by suggesting ways of linking works that connect with whatever themes and topics they are studying, with further links made with non-Western examples and art in the locality. The Y8 case study also illustrates how transferable the principles are. They can be used in relation to any gallery or museum collection, including those that are local and most accessible to schools.

The Content, Form, Process, Mood Model

The students' use of the Content, Form, Process, Mood model is crucial to this process. It asserts their right to conjecture and speculate in front of works of art by enabling them to pose a range of pertinent questions. The most fundamental ones to do with content are 'what is this work about? what is its meaning?' In terms of form, they should ask 'how has it been composed, arranged, designed?' Regarding process, 'how is it made, and what is it made of?' Mood is assessed by questioning, 'how is it affecting me, the viewer, and why?'

By using this model, both teachers and students can begin to make sense of, and respond to, art works, including those of which they have no prior knowledge. Their conjectures, of course, do not necessarily always provide answers. They can arouse a desire to know more, though! I am aware of many teachers and students researching from art books with a sense of excitement and urgency born of the desire to know more and to see if their interpretations are affirmed by others. By this means, the students are acquiring a form of knowledge that, in the first instance, is based on sensory responses of an aesthetic nature, as opposed to the learning and memorising of facts and dates to do with art and artists. In art lessons, the 'knowledge' cart is too often put in front of the 'understanding' horse. This model enables students to acquire forms of knowledge that grow directly out of insight and understanding.

A Model for Empowerment

Properly applied, the Content, Form, Process, Mood model is highly empowering. Nina, an A level student, uses it constantly. Her interest in feminine issues led her to choose Amanda Faulkner as one of the artists in her Personal Study. She admits to being 'physically repulsed by the vulgar images set down on the paper' on first seeing the painting *Mona*. She suggests that perhaps the title derives from Leonardo's *Mona Lisa*, an icon of female beauty, and that the artist deliberately made her woman ugly 'to get away from the traditional art stereotype women who are idealistically beautiful'. She feels Faulkner achieves this with devastating force in a work that is perhaps equally a comment on idealisation in the treatment of the mother and child theme. The figure on the right, possibly a child, wears a dress:

> 'From the dress hangs the right breast, it appears sharp and penetratingly frightening, the nipple is portrayed as piercing and pointed . . . The left breast also hangs out of the top of the bodice, but is rounded and appears stretched. Amanda emphasises the stretching by making slashing directional lines in blood red towards the nipple, possibly portraying an aspect of motherhood . . .'

Her face is flat and mask-like, 'as if hiding the true identity of the child', but:

> 'Maybe the mask-like face is representative of Amanda when she was a child . . . This childlike figure may be indicative of aspects in her life and her problems as a child going through puberty . . . Amanda shows the child in a dress and also out of it, like a discarded skin. The breast emerges, symbolising the new woman. The breasts are depicted as ugly, possibly signifying Amanda's reaction to her own development and therefore she sees these sexual organs as ugly and intimidating.'

She holds onto a flowing, washed-out pink ribbon on the dress. Perhaps this was used to tie up her pigtails, and shows 'Amanda's reluctance to let go of her childhood, and the faded colour signifies her childhood draining away as she goes through the physical metamorphosis into adulthood'. As a young adolescent herself, Nina constructs an extraordinary narrative that possibly contains autobiographical overtones.

Narrative Related to Life Experience

Neil MacGregor suggests that the current vogue for depopulated landscapes painted in and around Paris during a short period in the 19th century is because: 'As soon as you get people in a picture, you raise problems of narrative and meaning. And as soon as you raise questions of meaning, most of us feel we are at a disadvantage and might Get it Wrong'. He puts this down, at least in part, to a recent shift of emphasis in criticism away from emotional significance to visual pleasure, marking a fundamental change in the way people think about works of art: 'What has got lost is the idea that, when you look at a picture and you don't know what's going on in it, in a sense it doesn't matter whether you get it right or wrong. We should have the confidence to construct the narrative and decipher it in terms of our own experience.' The Content, Form, Process, Mood model does not deny the importance of visual pleasure but it also encourages students to construct narratives in terms of their experience, and this is exactly what Nina did with *Mona*. Another advantage of students being encouraged to respond to art works 'in the round' in these ways is the wonderfully varied use of language it stimulates. There is no richer place in a school in oracy terms than an art department which has these critical studies strategies firmly in place and is making daily use of them!

Connecting Theory and Practice

Nina also illustrates the important part this model plays in helping her to see and make connections between the artists she is studying and her own practice:

> 'The idea used in the Art History Course of using Form, Content, Mood and Process to analyse paintings is very good. This helps me to understand paintings better, even ones I have not seen before. Learning about art feeds my imagination for my practical work; it informs me about colour combinations, structures of pictures, techniques, and subject matter . . . Showing painters' Art Work also gives me insight to problems that may occur in my work (i.e. design fault) and by showing how the painter gets around the problems he or she has encountered helps me too.'

In this Personal Appraisal, Nina demonstrates she can make a whole web of connections between other artists' work and her own. Unlike Janet, as an A-level student, Nina is being challenged practically because she knows how to connect her 'excited discoveries' to her own practical needs in clear, systematic ways. With all these factors in mind, each of the following chapters tries to balance questions of a wide-ranging nature with the imparting of information. The questions are wide-ranging in that they fully encompass the four areas of content, form, process and mood; alert readers will rapidly work out into which category each one belongs.

A quantum leap will be achieved in art education when a majority of students leave school having gained an understanding and insight into a wide variety of art works, which they have acquired through direct engagement with them in interactive practical contexts. National Curriculum Art makes this a real possibility for the first time by emphasising the entitlement right of all students to an education that brings together requirements from both **Investigating and Making** and **Knowledge and Understanding**. 'Understanding and Investigating Art', as its title infers, directly addresses this issue, and will, I hope, make a worthwhile contribution to the process.

Rod Taylor
1997

THE HUMAN FIGURE

Identity and Relationships

What does it feel like to be a small burrowing creature under the ground, a four-legged beast bounding across the prairie, or a bird flying freely in space unimpeded by machinery or equipment? These ideas excite the imagination, but despite all our scientific knowledge we can still only wonder about them. We do know what it feels like to be a human being, however. Our humanity shapes all our feelings, thoughts and sensations. The sculptor, Henry Moore, maintained, 'If we were like horses who could go to sleep on all fours, all our architecture, all our art, would be different. Of course it would'. Your sense of scale and proportion is determined by your size and shape, and how you sit, move and walk. You can empathise and identify with the people you encounter in art, and share in their experiences. You can recognise characteristics in them that you see in the people you know, or are conscious you possess yourself. The **Human Figure** must be the first Universal Theme to be considered: as Moore insisted, 'If you don't learn from your own body, you'll learn from nothing'.

Personal Identity

Each of us is unique. We possess individual personality traits and physical attributes that give us our particular identities. What makes you distinctive? Consider which important experiences in your life have affected how you think, feel and act now. Everyone reflects on past experiences; try to recall your earliest memories. Inevitably, some phases of your life will be clearer than others, and you probably dwell on some moments more frequently than others. Equally, there may be some you prefer not to think about. Some past experiences will shape your future behaviour, and your hopes for the future are probably influenced by earlier experiences and by what is happening to you now. To what extent are your ambitions and aspirations shaped by experiences in your life to date?

An Allegory of Prudence

There is a Latin phrase at the top of *An Allegory of Prudence* which means, 'From the past the man of the present acts prudently so as not to imperil the future'. Titian painted this work near the end of an extremely long working life. A prudent person is careful, wise, sensible and far-sighted. How do the three male heads in this painting illustrate this allegory? The inscription is arranged in three parts relating to each head in turn. On the left is the aged Titian himself. The central portrait is believed to be that of his son Orazio. The youth on the right could be Marco Vecellio, who was born in 1545. Try to estimate the age of each person.

Titian's date of birth is unknown, but he died in 1576. Assuming Marco was born in 1545, how long before his death did Titian paint this picture? Assuming both your estimates are accurate, try to guess Titian's age when he died. According to some estimates, he was 99 years old and still painting when he died of the plague!

The painting could be of three generations – a grandparent, father and son. Or it may represent the same person at key stages in his life, perhaps a man reflecting on his youth. Could the inscription apply equally to three stages in one man's life, or to three generations, each influenced by the experiences of his predecessors?

Whether or not the heads represent one person or three different people may be irrelevant. They may, instead, symbolise different characteristics. A prudent act combines memory and intelligence with foresight, and each head could represent one of these qualities.

Produce a time-based autobiographical work of your own. Design it to represent three stages in your life: one as you are now, one of your past and one anticipating your future. Try to say something about your present frame of mind and your temperament and personality, as well as recording your outward appearance.

Focus on an incident that stands out clearly in your mind. Have you changed your interests much since then? Ask friends and relatives what you were like then compared with how they see you today.

In the third part project your mind into the future and represent yourself as you anticipate you will become. Think about the lifestyle you would like. How do you anticipate fashions will change and how will you respond to them? Perhaps you have an older relative whose life may provide you with a glimpse of your possible future self.

What colours, rhythms, shapes or textures are most expressive of your personality? Do they differ from those you associate with your younger self? Try to use these formal elements to give strength and unity to your design. Your painting is about the impact of time on your life, devote the whole picture area to the theme. Try to find appropriate ways of interconnecting the three versions of yourself into one unified design, and look at how Titian solved both these problems.

Tiziano Vecellio, called Titian, Italian (active about 1506, died 1576)
An Allegory of Prudence, (about 1567–70)
Oil on Canvas (76.2 × 68.6 cm)

Variations in Stone and Iron

Titian indicates one way of connecting three phases of your life. Compare his allegory with three stone carved figures on the façade of Laon Cathedral in France. One complete figure, head in hands, is in the centre. He is flanked by two large heads, both looking away from him. How much older do you think the bearded man on the right is to the one on the left? Think about what is causing the central figure to bury his head in his hands. Does he look frightened, distressed, in pain, or lost in thought? Try to work out whether any relationship, psychological or formal, links the figures. Perhaps they are simply three separate people with nothing in common.

In representing three phases of your life, you might feel the contrast between a smaller central figure and two portrait heads offers variety and contrast. If this variation appeals to you, consider which phase of your life can most effectively be expressed through the whole figure.

Laon Cathedral, West Front (12th century Gothic)
Stone carving

A detail from the cast iron and copper gate of the Liverpool Philharmonic Hotel, designed by H. Bloomfield Bone in 1900, shows a front-facing female head positioned above two profile ones. Do the hairstyles and features suggest that all three heads show the same person from different angles?

Gate, The Liverpool Philharmonic Hotel, Liverpool, England (1900)
Iron and copper

Even though the profile heads face away from each other, it is difficult not to sense a relationship between them. The curving rhythms of the ironwork make your eye study each head in turn as you follow the flowing design. The rhythms create a relationship that links all the three heads, but if they were of different women, would you still sense the relationships as strongly? You may prefer to show your own three portraits physically apart but rhythmically related like these. Think about which head best represents particular phases in your life.

Autobiography and Self-Portraiture

We know more about ourselves than anyone else, however close we might be to them. Your body, and your most private, innermost thoughts and feelings, are your ever-present companions. However much you might want to, you cannot escape from them. It is hardly surprising, therefore, that so many artists produce self-portraits at some stage in their careers. Self-portraits capture not only a single moment in time, but can also inform us about an artist's life in a wider sense. Consider whether artists are able to say as much about their lives through self-portraiture as authors do in autobiographies. Is a self-portrait a unique statement about personal identity, whatever additional concerns the artist might be addressing?

Are you aware of the identity of any artists through their self-portraits? Some are well known enough to appear on calendars, tee-shirts, mugs, postcards, reproductions and gift cards. Some people who do not visit art galleries still recognise van Gogh and Rembrandt because their self-portraits are so widely available.

Self-Portrait at the Age of 63

One pub sign in Manchester shows the head and shoulders of an elderly man. Two distinctive tufts of hair sprout from under his white edged beret. His face looks tired and care-worn, but his gaze is unerring.

The pub is the 'Rembrandt'. The image on the sign resembles Rembrandt's *Self-Portrait at the Age of 63* in the National Gallery, closely enough to suggest it could be based on it. The background is olive green, though, and Rembrandt rarely used green in its own right. If *Self-Portrait at the Age of 63* is typical, what colours does Rembrandt seem to prefer?

Rembrandt Pub Sign, Manchester, England

Rembrandt's use of tone is equally distinctive: Look at how much canvas area is in light tones and how much of it is dark. Rembrandt used highlights very skilfully. In this picture the highlights on the face suggest a spotlight picking out details on an actor's face, with the rest of the stage in darkness. This use of light and shade is called *chiaroscuro*, from an Italian word meaning 'light-dark'.

The Italian artist, Caravaggio, (see page 99) was famous for his use of chiaroscuro, being one of the first to exaggerate the contrast between dark areas and highlights for dramatic ends. Rembrandt never went to Italy, but was indirectly influenced by Caravaggio. Chiaroscuro was introduced into Dutch painting by Dutch artists who did visit Italy.

Try to imagine what kind of person Rembrandt was. Look carefully at his features. Allow your eye to travel from such features as eyes and nose to the many wrinkles and lines that mark his face. Does he paint himself honestly, warts and all, or do you think he is unable to resist the temptation to idealise and flatter himself?

Imagine nothing is recorded or known about Rembrandt's life, but that you know him. What is he like? Is he humorous and cheerful or a pessimist? What are his likes and dislikes? Using the clues in this painting as the basis, write a short biography about him. Describe his lifestyle and the events in his life that have affected the way he looks now in this, the last year of his life.

Harmensz. van Rijn, called Rembrandt, Dutch (1606–1669)
Self-Portrait at the Age of 63 (1669)
Oil on Canvas (86 × 70.5 cm)

Self-Portrait at the Age of 34

Make sure, though, that you also take full account of the clues in another of Rembrandt's self-portraits, painted when he was much younger. *Self-Portrait at the Age of 34*, with its distinctive curved top, hangs on the opposite wall in the National Gallery. Compare them, moving from one to the other, looking at their differences and similarities. Do you think that Rembrandt's outlook on life has changed in the intervening 29 years? Think about the changes that have occurred and describe the two states of mind you see reflected in these paintings. Does his clothing at 34 contrast with what he chooses to wear in old age? A dramatic change has obviously taken place in his lifestyle between 1640 and 1669. What has caused this?

Harmensz. van Rijn, called Rembrandt, Dutch (1606–1669)
Self-Portrait at the Age of 34 (1640)
Oil on Canvas (102 × 80 cm)

Portrait of a Man

Rembrandt drew on the works of artists he admired. Compare the pose of *Self-Portrait at the Age of 34* with that in Titian's *Portrait of a Man*. The close resemblance tells you unmistakably that Titian is an artist Rembrandt greatly admired. Each sitter looks straight at us, but both poses are sideways-on. How is the right arm resting on the parapet important to the design of these paintings? Focus on the texture and shape of the man's sleeve in the Titian portrait, and consider which is the most important feature in the composition, the portrait or the magnificent sleeve. Is the sleeve similarly prominent in the Rembrandt self-portrait?

Rembrandt obviously deliberately chose a similar pose to that in the Titian, possibly because he was consciously paying homage to an artist he admired. Compare the colour schemes of the two paintings. They differ greatly, but are they similar in any way? Colour significantly affects the mood of both paintings. Do you think Rembrandt is copying an idea of Titian's because he has none of his own, or does Titian's example help him create a unique work of his own? Consider the differences between reworking and reinterpreting an idea, as opposed to simply copying. Sometimes artists do copy existing works. What is the purpose of this?

Think about your favourite artists and whether they influence your work in any way. If they do, how does your work benefit? A growing awareness of art and artists can help your own work develop in many helpful and unexpected ways. Similarly, the problems and concerns you deal with in your work can increase your appreciation of artists who deal with related issues.

Recreate the above poses by sitting sideways on to a mirror. Rest your right arm horizontally on a flat surface and turn your head till you make eye contact with your reflected gaze. How conscious are you of the twist in your body? As well as simply looking at your reflection, how physically aware are you of bodily movement and sensation? How does posing like this affect different parts of your body? Would it occur to you to assume a pose like this without the example of Rembrandt and Titian?

You are recreating a pose from art history in real life. How is this different to simply copying the Rembrandt or the Titian?

Tiziano Vecellio, called Titian, Italian (active about 1506, died 1576)
Portrait of a Man (about 1512)
Oil on Canvas (81.2 × 66.3 cm)

Portrait of a Young Man

Being an artist demands the use of all your senses. These are equally necessary for you to respond fully to other artists' work. In *Portrait of a Young Man*, Andrea del Sarto chose an even more exaggerated pose to convey sensations involving twisting bodily movement. The man looks directly at us, but to do so he must literally look over his left shoulder. Re-enact this pose, looking at yourself over one shoulder and into a mirror. You can probably feel the more exaggerated twist of this pose through every part of your body. We have to 'feel' poses of this nature in addition to simply seeing them.

Recording Bodily Movement

Experiment by making rapid sketches of yourself in poses that require twisting movements. Try to reconcile the physical sensations you experience with what you can see while drawing or painting. Encourage friends and members of your family to develop the habit of posing for you from time to time. Get them to adopt poses full of movement and vitality. Work rapidly – poses like this cannot be held for long. Help your models to be conscious of the kinds of rhythmical movement you want them to achieve while posing.

Record family and friends moving about in everyday situations. Photograph them and if you have access to a camcorder, ask a friend to sit down, move through a range of positions, and then stand up again. Record and analyse key stages in it by playing the film back at both normal and slow speeds. Use the freeze frame to study particularly interesting moments more closely. Observe people's actions while watching television, and video interesting sequences to scrutinise them.

As well as painting, Rembrandt produced hundreds of rapid sketches of people. He found pen, ink and wash the ideal media with which to record such subjects. What media do you use when sketching? Are you willing to experiment with new ones or fresh combinations of those you already use?

Clay is an ideal medium in which to represent poses. Working rapidly, without paying any attention to 'finish', try building a figure ensuring that each piece of clay you add clarifies a particular movement. Always carry a small sketchbook with you to enable you to make rapid sketches recording the actions and movements of people going about their daily business.

Andrea del Sarto, Italian (1486–1530)
Portrait of a Young Man (about 1517–18)
Oil on Linen (72.4 × 57.2 cm)

Self-Portrait in a Straw Hat

Make full use of yourself as a model. Endless variations are possible. It is interesting to compare two self-portraits, one by the 18th century French artist Elizabeth Vigée Le Brun, the other by the 17th century Spaniard, Bartolomé Murillo (see page 22). Have you ever thought of dressing yourself up or, though working indoors, of imaginatively painting a picture of yourself out-of-doors? Vigée Le Brun does both these things in *Self-Portrait in a Straw Hat*. This painting is a replica of an earlier version painted in 1782, now in Brussels. Most artistic representations of women are seen through men's eyes. On the evidence of this painting, consider whether there are significant differences in the way a woman chooses to represent herself compared with how a man might depict her. The painting provides clues about Vigée Le Brun's personality. Consider whether she is a hesitant person or someone confident in her artistic abilities and proud of her talent. Does she look as if she is the kind of woman who averts her gaze or makes direct eye contact with you when you meet her?

The painting was done in the studio, but Vigée Le Brun shows herself outside standing against a blue sky flecked with pink-edged grey clouds. Where is the horizon line showing where landscape meets sky? Is it where you would expect to find it? Does setting herself against sky, rather than landscape, make Vigée Le Brun seem more or less imposing?

Get a friend to stand in bright sunlight wearing a broad-brimmed hat. Examine the contrast between the flesh in sunlight and the shadow the hat casts on the face and compare it with the kind of contrast used by Vigée Le Brun. She may have modified the contrast. Try to decide whether it is stronger or softer and why she altered it.

Vigée Le Brun's clothes and demeanour provide important clues about her social status. Consider whether she is really dressed for painting in oils, or whether she has chosen her clothes to convey a particular image. They may be from a 'prop' cupboard rather than her own wardrobe. If they are her clothes, when might she wear them? Think about how she uses them to present herself in the painting, and which items of clothing are most eye-catching. What is your reaction to her overall appearance?

Elizabeth Louise Vigée Le Brun, French (1755–1842)
Self-Portrait in a Straw Hat (after 1782)
Oil on Canvas (97.8 × 70.5 cm)

Self-Portrait

How geometrical is the design of Murillo's *Self-Portrait*? An oval frame almost fills the rectangle of the canvas. Murillo's black coat and hair merge into the background, but the light picks out his face and white collar. The oval frame may be a mirror. If it is, how does Murillo manage to place his hand on the frame in front of the reflection? If it is not a mirror, how is he able to see himself? Is he holding an empty picture frame? If so, does this mean the whole scene must be reflected in a much larger mirror? He deliberately wanted to puzzle us. Having demonstrated he can paint reality so convincingly, he is perhaps emphasising that all art is only an illusion of reality.

Murillo's palette and brushes rest on the ledge to the right of the picture, slanting towards him. Erika Langmuir points out: 'The white on the palette is a real, three-dimensional swirl of white lead paint, not the image of one'! Is this a further reminder that painting is an illusion? The other 'tools of the profession' correspondingly slant in from the left, and everything leads our eye to the centrally framed artist. In addition to a red chalk drawing, the items include the chalk itself, a ruler and a pair of dividers. They are intended to show what a learned artist he is, a man capable of using measurement and proportion effectively, as well as producing good pictures.

Beneath the mirror is a tablet with a Latin inscription which means: 'Bartolomé Murillo portraying himself to fulfil the wishes and prayers of his children'. Only four of his nine children were still alive by 1670 when the painting was executed.

Look at the palette in Murillo's Self-Portrait *and compare it with the one Vigée Le Brun is holding. Are his colours set out in any order? Why do you think Vigée Le Brun and Murillo set their paints out in the way they do? The two paintings are very different in their use of colour. Which do you prefer and why?*

- *Is there any connection between the colour schemes used and the colours set out on the palettes within them?*

- *How would you describe each colour scheme?*

- *Do the paintings differ much in mood? What effect do the colour schemes have on the mood of each painting?*

- *Which words best capture the atmosphere and spirit of each painting?*

- *Is Murillo as confident and proud of his artistic abilities and status as Vigée Le Brun is of hers? The muted, restricted colour range he favours may seem dull, but it is used to effectively capture the mood of sober dignity that he wanted to achieve.*

Bartolomé Esteban Murillo, Spanish (1617–1682)
Self-Portrait (probably 1670–3)
Oil on Canvas (122 × 107 cm)

'Le Chapeau de Paille'

In 'Le Chapeau de Paille', the Flemish artist Rubens painted a portrait of his sister-in-law, Susanna Lunden. It is in the National Gallery, and it, too, shows a half length woman in a broad brimmed hat set against the sky, with most of her face in shadow. The title means *The Straw Hat*. Compare it with Vigée Le Brun's painting. Vigée Le Brun based her self-portrait on this painting, just as Rembrandt used a design by Titian. We know for certain that Vigée Le Brun admired the Rubens. She wrote that the great effect of 'Le Chapeau de Paille' 'resides in the two different kinds of illumination which simple daylight and the light of the sun create'. The painting inspired her 'to the point that I made my own portrait . . . in search of the same effect'. Interestingly, Vigée Le Brun wears a real straw hat, embellished with flowers. Compare it to the hat in 'Le Chapeau de Paille'. Is this a straw hat, as the title suggests? If it is not, what is it made of? Examine the difference in the way Rubens, a male artist, paints an attractive woman and how Vigée Le Brun, a female artist, depicts herself in a similar pose and context. Which do you prefer and why?

The psychological aspects of self-portraiture make it a fascinating genre. Think about what you want to say about yourself, and if there is anything you wish to conceal. You can embellish and change your appearance by dressing in a particular way, like Vigée Le Brun. If you have ever worn a stage costume and make-up, you may remember that it brought out aspects of your personality you were not usually aware of. Personal adornment is increasingly accepted as appropriate to both young men and women. Dressing up for a special occasion, like Vigée Le Brun did, can help you bring out aspects of your nature and temperament you might not otherwise address.

Try, therefore, to say something important about yourself as a person in addition to recording your outward appearance. Your favourite clothes or some personal possessions might help to emphasise aspects of your personality. They may relate to hobbies and interests, or reflect your ambitions. Find an area of your home you particularly like because of its colour scheme, decorative detail or mood, and think about whether this is the best environment in which to represent yourself. Make a self-portrait that takes full account of these and similar considerations.

Peter Paul Rubens, Flemish (1577–1640)
Portrait of Susanna Lunden(?) ('Le Chapeau de Paille')
(probably 1622–5)
Oil on Oak (79 × 54.6 cm)

The examples considered so far show sitters making direct eye contact with the viewer. Eye contact usually helps to identify more closely with the model. Some people feel comfortable and relaxed in the person's presence, but others feel disturbed and inhibited by eye contact and may wish to avert their gaze.

Other angles feature in portraiture. If you collect postage stamps, cameos or coins, the most common alternative to frontal and three-quarter views will already be in your mind: the profile. Ancient Greek and Roman coins were widely collected during the Renaissance. Imagine you were alive centuries before the advent of television, film and photography. Would you be interested in the actual appearance of people famous enough for you to know about them, even though they lived around 1500 years ago?

Cameo Portrait of Augustus

People had an idea of what Roman emperors like Caesar, Agrippa, Nero and Caligula looked like from coins. Augustus ruled at the time of Christ. He appears on a cameo wearing the protective shield of the god Zeus. The heads of Phobos, representing Fear, and Medusa (see page 137) can be seen on his shield. To emphasise his nobility and importance, Augustus has a classical Grecian profile, and wears a jewelled diadem on his head. This was actually added later, possibly replacing a laurel wreath. What is a cameo? How does an artist achieve different colours within the same cameo design?

How conscious do you think people were of their own profiles in the 15th century? Are you more conscious of yours today because photography has made you more aware of what you look like from different angles? Make a coiled clay model of your head relying on your sense of touch for information.

Explore your features and the form, structure and shape of your head using your fingers. Run your fingers up and down your nose, chin, forehead and round the back of your head. What does your profile feel like? Utilise all this data to represent yourself fully in the round.

When you have done so, search out any photographs you can find of yourself in profile or near-profile positions and compare them with the profile of your sculpture. How reliable did your sense of touch prove to be? Do you need to modify your sculpture in any way in the light of this new visual evidence?

*Portrait of Augustus
Sardonyx Cameo, (H12.8 cm)
Courtesy of the Trustees of the
British Museum*

Portrait of a Lady in Yellow

The profile enjoys a long history in European portraiture. A striking example is *Portrait of a Lady in Yellow* by Alesso Baldovinetti. Compare this with the reality Murillo achieved in 'Self-Portrait'. Profile views often possess a more linear quality that emphasises the outline shape of the head. Follow the outline of the woman. Start with her sleeve at the lower edge of the painting. Allow your eye to travel all the way round her until it returns to the opposite lower edge. Is it a graceful, rhythmical and lyrical journey or a straightforward, predictable one?

As you follow the curve of the lady's neck, nose, forehead and top of her head, think about what the outline tells you about her. It is so clean and crisp all the way round, it is easy to follow. The contrast between the pale amber and straw colours of the woman and the plain blue background ensures this. The effect is further heightened because Baldovinetti does not choose to use any strong contrasts of light and shade. Could you follow the outline of a Rembrandt self-portrait as easily in the same way?

Three palms are stitched on the lady's sleeve. They make a bold pattern, but could also signify something important like a family coat of arms. As yet, nobody has been able to identify who she is.

You may find Portrait of a Lady in Yellow *rather flat and two-dimensional. Do you think Baldovinetti's main concern is to emphasise the two-dimensional outline because this is what he finds most attractive? Do any details stand out because they are more three-dimensional in treatment? Can you sense form in the way he paints the eye and socket for example? Does he make the four pearls on top of her head look convincingly three-dimensional?*

Study them closely, using a hand lens if you have one, and look at how he achieved the highlights on them. Look for similar small dots of paint elsewhere. You will certainly find some on her face and dress, particularly to suggest form on the folds of the sleeve. Baldovinetti also uses them to indicate light and shade on her hairband. Do these help to make her head look more three-dimensional than would otherwise be the case? Were you aware of this subtle 'pointillist' modelling when you first looked at the painting? Think about whether it helps the artist achieve three-dimensional effects where he wants them, even though his primary concern appears to be with the more two-dimensional qualities.

Alesso Baldovinetti, Italian (about 1426–1499)
Portrait of a Lady in Yellow (probably 1465)
Tempera and Oil on Wood (62.9 × 40.6 cm)

She wears expensive-looking jewellery, her dress is made out of rich material and her bearing is dignified. Assuming it is a coat of arms on the sleeve, who might she be? She looks rather remote and passive. Is she always like this or does she only seem remote because she is looking straight ahead and therefore away from us? Rulers and heads of state are deliberately shown in profile on coins and stamps to make them seem remote and therefore more imposing and dignified. Consider whether a profile view says more or less about a person's character than a portrait of someone looking straight at you.

The Profile in Non-Western Art

Compare the relief of the armed Persian bodyguard of Darius the Great with the Egyptian nobleman Nebamon (see page 83). He was originally one of many forming a frieze on the palace of Darius, made entirely of glazed bricks. How does the colour on the bodyguard ensure he stands out from his background. Compare the colour of the Immortal and his background with Baldovinetti's 'Lady in Yellow' and her background. They are in different media but share some important similarities.

Bodyguard, Palace of Darius, Persia [Iran]
Relief of polychrome bricks (H 147 cm)
Courtesy of the Trustees of the British Museum

Portrait of Shan Jahan holding a seal engraved with his titles

This is an Indian Mogul miniature. Compare its size with the National Gallery portraits you have studied, and think about how miniatures were meant to be seen.

Using the measurements of the painting as a basis, work out what size the central oval shape is in the original. Draw it that size and place Shan Jahan within it. Are you surprised at how small he actually is? Try to work out his age. Does two years older than Rembrandt in his earlier self-portrait seem about right? He is an Indian emperor, and his clothes emphasise his status. What are seals like this used for and why would Shan Jahan regard his as important?

The whole painting is highly embellished. Does the elaborate decoration and detail detract from Shan Jahan or help you focus on him? The decorative borders might tell you more about Shan Jahan. The outer border is filled with detailed plant studies. Have you seen similar botanical studies? Where do you normally expect to see studies like these? Imagine the portrait without its surroundings and enlarged to the size of *Portrait of a Lady in Yellow*. Would it be more or less interesting? Shan Jahan's red dress contrasts with a green background, much as the blond colours of the lady in yellow contrast with the blue background. The portrait oval is set within a central rectangle, leaving four distinctive corner shapes. The patterns in them resemble those on oriental carpets. Calligraphy often features in Islamic art and the inner border contains writing. What do you imagine it says? Does Shan Jahan look approachable or aloof?

Choose a person you know. Change the status of the person by imagining (s)he is important enough to be represented on coins and stamps. What kind of bearing would this person need to assume to appear appropriately dignified? How would you hold your head if you had to be depicted as a ruler on a coin?

Make a series of profile studies and use these as the basis for a profile portrait. Incorporate this into a design which also includes borders and surrounds or additional decorative detail of some kind. Make these as attractive as possible in their own right, but consider how they might also tell the viewer something additional about the person. What interests and concerns motivate this person? What kind of temperament and personality characterises him or her?

Try to convey as much as you can about this person through the motifs you choose, as well as through the portrait itself. A unified design helps to ensure that all the elements contribute to the overall design and effect of the work.

Portrait of Shan Jahan holding a seal engraved with his title,
India (18th century)
Mogul Miniature (19 ×14 cm)
Courtesy of the Trustees of the British Museum

Pope Julius II

A person can face us, yet still choose not to make eye contact, of course. Raphael's *Portrait of Pope Julius II* does just this. You can sense his power and authority, but would he seem as powerful if he looked straight at you? Raphael achieves such a sense of reality and human presence that the Italian painter and biographer Vasari described this portrait as being 'so lifelike and true it frightened everyone who saw it, as if it were the living man himself'. Do you think Raphael persuaded Pope Julius to assume this pose or do you think he always sat like this? Imagine you are inside the same room standing alongside Pope Julius, and think about whether you would feel relaxed or uncomfortable and in awe of him. Would he continue to look away from you and ignore you? Would you dare to speak to him without him first addressing you? Note the incline of his head, and observe his eyes and the set of his mouth, and try to imagine what he is thinking and feeling.

The bold colour scheme is in red, green and white. Look at how these colours are organised and how much of the picture area each one occupies? Do you think they make an effective combination? How do they contribute to the overall impact of the work? Do you find Raphael's treatment of textures like the ermine edging of the Pope's robe and cap, his tassels and white linen robe convincing? There are cross keys on the green wallpaper, and gilt acorns adorn each arm of his papal throne. What do you think these might signify?

Raphael's Pope Julius II *exerted a profound influence on portraiture. Cover the Pope's head so you can focus solely on his hands. Have they got character? Are they those of the same old man whose portrait you are studying? Do they tell you anything additional about him?*

Observe how one hand tightly grips the arm of the throne and the other clasps a handkerchief.

Study peoples' hands. What do different people do with their hands when they sit down and relax? Do they fold or clasp them together? Do they do different things with each hand?

Make separate drawings of the heads and hands of people of varying ages supported, where possible, by photographs. Mix these together and then 'rematch' the hands with the correct faces. Think about whether hands are as expressive of age as faces, and whether they show character and personality as clearly. Arrange the hands according to the age of each person. Is similar evidence of ageing revealed in the sequence of the hands as in the heads?

Raffaello Sanzio, called Raphael, Italian (1483–1520)
Pope Julius II (1511–12)
Oil on Wood (108 × 80.7 cm)

Madame Moitessier

Madame Moitessier, completed by Ingres in 1856, is a distinctive example. What strikes you first when you look at this portrait? It may be the strangely-positioned fingers of her right hand. Her index finger is particularly eye-catching in the way it is outstretched, lightly touching the side of her head. You may have noticed how some people carefully raise their little finger in order to look elegant while holding a cup of tea. Does this raised finger help to make Madame Moitessier look more elegant and refined? If her hand was resting in her lap like the one holding the fan, would this significantly alter the mood of the work? Compare the tone of her flesh with the white of her dress. Do any brushstrokes show in this painting? Look at the geometrical shapes Ingres employed to organise Madame Moitessier's dress, head and arms. Notice how he organised the painting in terms of dark and light areas. By what means does he introduce darker tones into the lighter areas, and vice-versa?

How long were you looking at *Madame Moitessier* before you became aware that a profile view is also included? It is reflected in the mirror on the right. What colour does Ingres use to link this profile to the main portrait? Does her profile seem to emerge out of its darker surroundings or blend into them? Does her jewellery, chintz dress and surroundings suggest to you she is wealthy?

You are already aware of Madame Moitessier's distinctive right hand. Do you ever place a hand against your face? When you are deep in thought, are you likely to rest your chin in your hand? Do you occasionally even place a finger in your mouth? If so, which finger is it? Can you think of any other situations in which you bring your hands into contact with your face? A common reaction to grief, for example, is for people to bury their heads in their hands.

Make a series of studies that explore the relationship between heads and hands. Sit in front of a mirror and experiment with your hands in relation to your face, imagining yourself in a variety of emotional situations and contexts. Tense and extend your fingers in various ways. Do some situations cause you to modify your posture and make you feel differently about yourself? Get a friend to pose, making hand movements and gestures denoting varying degrees of status and importance. Photograph and sketch these. Look at what certain gestures and positions of the hand in relationship to the face show. See how wide a range of statements to do with status and different emotions you can generate between you. Were you previously aware how expressive your hands were in relation to your head?

Jean-Auguste-Dominique Ingres, French (1780–1867)
Madame Moitessier (1856)
Oil on Canvas (120 × 92.1 cm)

Ingres is described as a **Neo-Classical** artist, and he emphasises her classical Grecian profile. Is this similar to the one of Augustus you have already seen on the cameo? What does **Neo-Classical** mean? Are any other classical references included in the painting? Madame Moitessier was 35 when Ingres completed this painting, but he spent nine years working on it. Try to imagine what she looked like when she was only 26, and think about whether Ingres changed the painting much over the nine year period.

Experiment by sitting a friend in front of a mirror in a similar pose. Alter your own position by moving around. Try and find a position from which you can see your model both frontally and in profile as Ingres does Madame Moitessier. However you position yourself, do you not find that the sitter still obscures part of her reflection? In order to show her frontally and in profile most effectively, Ingres modifies what is literally there. He uses 'artistic licence' to help him achieve his desired ends.

The Human Body as Subject Matter

You have already seen how some artists use the body as an essential part of portraiture. The human body is an important subject in its own right, though, with a very long history of its own. For centuries, artists have studied the nude model as an essential part of their training. For some, the human body is such an expressive and formally interesting subject that they choose to explore its possibilities throughout their whole lives.

The Toilet of Venus

One of the best known examples of the female nude in the National Gallery is *The Toilet of Venus* by Velázquez. It is commonly known as *The Rokeby Venus* because it used to be in Rokeby Hall in Yorkshire. Velázquez is believed to have painted another version, but this work is unique. It is the only Spanish painting of the female nude produced prior to the 19th century still in existence today. Religious attitudes meant artists were discouraged from painting the female nude form.

Think about how, if at all, these constraints might have influenced Velázquez' choice of pose. The woman faces away from us, but gazes intently into a mirror. Do you think a back view might have been more acceptable to Velázquez' contemporaries than a frontal one with her looking at you, the viewer? Is it possible her reflected gaze is directed at you, the viewer, though? Do you think Velázquez nevertheless felt the need to soften the impact of her gaze by making her face slightly out-of-focus and bathed in shadow? A boyish winged Cupid holds the mirror for her, emphasising she is the goddess Venus and not just any woman. There is a long tradition of representing the female nude in mythological contexts. Velázquez may simply have wanted to paint an ordinary woman, though. Perhaps he called her Venus and added Cupid to make the work more acceptable to prudish minds. Cover up the Cupid with your hand. Is the woman still Venus or is she now just an ordinary person relaxing in her bedroom?

Consider the overall shape her body makes. Does Velázquez create a perfect form you find pleasing to the eye, or would you modify it in some way to make it more beautiful? Try to describe this shape. The flowing draperies surrounding her create long sensuous rhythms. Do you sense any relationship between these and those of her body? Does she fit naturally into her surroundings? Is the overall design of the painting rhythmically pleasing?

Look at how colour is organised in this painting. Are you surprised at the narrow range that are used? Do these work satisfactorily together? Velázquez makes the woman's body look rounded and three-dimensional.

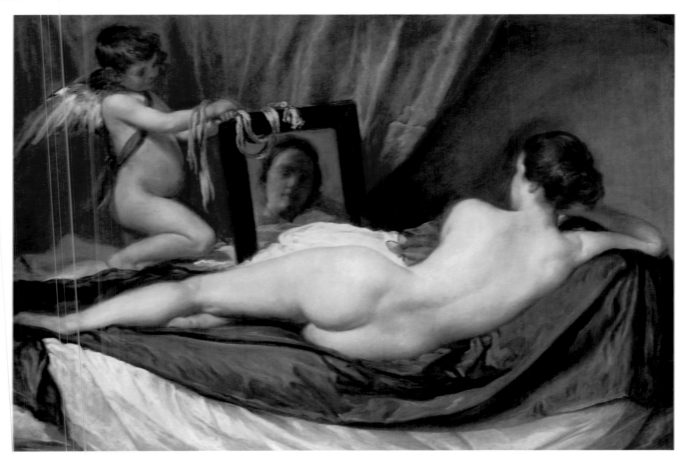

Compare The Rokeby Venus *with 'After the Bath, Woman drying herself' by Degas (page 33). Which treatment of the female body do you think is the more beautiful? Are the rhythms made by the body of Degas' woman similar or in marked contrast to those of Venus? How much of her head can you see? Just a glimpse of red hair shows above the towel as she bends over with her back turned to us, like the Venus. Degas feels no need to show us her face reflected in a* mirror, however. Venus reclines *gracefully on her right arm, looking dreamily into her mirror. What role does the right arm of the woman towelling herself play in the design of the painting and in the activity she is performing? Degas shows her absorbed in what she is doing. As a painter of 'modern life', he insisted this was his aim. Where Velázquez idealises his woman, calling her Venus, Degas emphasises that his woman is as ordinary as you and me.*

Diego Velázquez, Spanish (1599–1660)
The Toilet of Venus (The Rokeby Venus)
(1647–51)
Oil on Canvas
(122.5 × 177 cm)

Examine the technical means he uses to achieve this feeling of form. Notice how the brushwork successfully suggests the textures of flesh and the various materials surrounding Venus. The paleness of her flesh ensures that she stands out against the background. Flesh reflects light, and Velázquez has captured the translucency of her skin. He is often described as a 'painter's painter'. What do you think this phrase means? Erika Langmuir describes the 'single brushstroke laden with black paint, tracing the line that runs beneath her body from the middle of the back to below her calf', as 'even more astonishing' than the way Velázquez paints the flesh and the ribbons looping over the frame of the mirror!

After the Bath, Woman drying herself

Compare Degas' treatment of the woman's back with the fluid brushstrokes Velázquez uses on the back of Venus. Look at the bold vertical lines Degas left showing without attempting to smooth them together. Degas was a painter who loved to draw and make lines. *After the Bath* was executed in a medium that allowed him to paint in areas and patches of colour, and to draw at the same time. What media do you consider to be the most appropriate for this purpose? Pastel was Degas' preferred medium.

Study the picture surface and try to see whether Degas applied his pastel in the same technique or by using a wide variety of methods. Did his technique vary according to the nature of the surface, material or texture he is representing? What kind of surface do you think he worked on? Did he use just one piece or did he join a number of pieces together? When you visit the National Gallery, look closely at this pastel and see if you can work out how many pieces Degas used. Look at the way the pastel is applied on either side of the joins to see if you can tell which pieces were added after he had begun. Do you think Degas modified his compositions as he went along, or were they worked out in advance? Some artists prefer to apply paint smoothly, others apply it broadly, leaving each brushstroke showing. Degas made no attempt to conceal his methods of execution. Do you think the way the pastel is applied is essential to the conception of this painting?

Degas was working at the dawn of the photographic era. A photographer himself, he made use of photographic effects in his paintings. Can you find any evidence of the possible influence of photography in *After the Bath?* Though he uncannily achieves the kind of unexpected snapshot effects the camera reveals, was it actually technically possible to take 'snapshot' photographs 120 years ago? Could the pose of the woman, caught as if frozen in mid-movement as she towels her back, indicate the influence of photography?

Photography is taken for granted today. Large numbers of people take photographs. Camcorders that enable you to record activities in real time, are becoming increasingly commonplace. You have grown up in a world of photographic imagery, with the cinema, television and the photocopier. Maybe you already take virtual reality for granted. Imagine the kind of impact photography must have had on people's perceptions of the world when it was first introduced during the 19th century. In what other ways do you think artists might have been influenced by photography at that time?

Although Degas was influenced by photography, he did not normally work from photographs. How does he manage to capture split-second moments so exactly? It is said he had a photographic memory, but he also reconstructed the poses he wanted by using models in his studio.

Try to capture people frozen in mid-movement yourself. What additional aids are open to you today? In addition to your use of the sketchbook, use a video. Athletes and sportspeople make good subjects, but a sequence as basic as people walking will do. Use the freeze frame a number of times. Make a rapid study each time until you have recorded a number of stages of the same movement. Spread your drawings out. Select one for further development.

Using a medium like cray-pas or pastel, develop this drawing on a larger scale. Select a limited range of colours expressive of the mood you want. Pastel is ideal for the purpose. If you work on tinted paper, you might find it helpful to establish the main contours of your design by covering the paper in broad areas of wash. Work broadly and freely, but deliberately and precisely where appropriate. Notice how Degas laid one colour on top

of another to establish texture and enrich the picture surface. Observe how he merged colours into each other. Look at how decisively he put down a patch of colour or a stroke of the pastel – and then left it alone.

Hilaire-Germain-Edgar Degas, French
(1834–1917)
After the Bath, Woman drying herself
(probably 1888–92)
Pastel on Paper mounted on cardboard
(103.8 × 98.4 cm)

Family Relationships

Single portraits are about individual identity, but relationships that link people are equally important. You have already reflected on your early memories. Do these go back to when you were a baby? A baby starts life helpless and is obviously dependent on others. Its bonding with another person is crucial to its future relationships. Does this explain, at least in part, why the mother and child is such a recurrent theme in art? In Western art, of course, church patronage has also led to the production of numerous Virgin and Child paintings. A number hang in the National Gallery. Many are concerned with the initial bonding of a mother with her baby. The earliest examples are set against gold backgrounds, but later interpretations show the Christ child with his mother in all kinds of interior and even outdoor settings.

The Virgin and Child before a Firescreen

In this picture, a follower of Robert Campin placed the mother and child in a typical 15th century Flemish interior. At first glance, they look like any ordinary Netherlandish mother and baby of the time. Does their ordinariness detract from the religious significance of the painting? Think about whether the baby seems contented and whether the mother and child look as if they belong together and have 'bonded'. The firescreen referred to in the title is an eye-catching feature. What does its texture tell you it is made of? Why do you think the firescreen is included in the title? It might be because it is more than just a firescreen with additional symbolic significance. The more realistic Flemish paintings became, the more artists introduced symbols to indicate the religious significance of their subject matter. Do you find this painting convincingly realistic? Are there any other objects in it that might also be important symbols?

The Virgin's dress is an unusual pale colour. It was richer when it was first painted. Consider why it has faded, and why some colours fade more than others. Campin obviously enjoyed painting the surfaces and textures of things. Look at the texture of the Virgin's hair and her sleeve cuffs. What other textual surfaces do you find particularly interesting? What kind of day do you think it is? The tongues of flame that show above the firescreen suggest it could be a cool day and the baby needs extra warmth. A window is open, though, and the breeze is strong enough to cause a page of an open book to flutter. What do you think this book is? It looks like a bible, but if it is why do you think Campin included it?

Do you think the floor tiles of The Virgin and Child before a Firescreen *are square or rectangular? They lead your eye to the far wall of the room. Sooner or later, it is inevitably drawn to the distant townscape, visible through the window. Does this add extra depth and a feeling of space to the picture?*

- *Describe the view, including all its detail. Use a hand lens to help you. Do you think Campin used a hand lens to enable him to paint in such detail?*

- *Is anything going on in the townscape?*

- *Do you think the townscape adds to the painting, or does it form a separate picture within a picture?*

- *Cover the townscape over with your hand. Does its absence alter the mood of the painting?*

- *Does the townscape improve the painting or would you prefer the picture without any view at all?*

**Follower of Campin, Netherlandish
(Campin 1378/9–1444)**
*The Virgin and Child before a Firescreen,
(probably about 1440)*
Oil on Oak
(63.5 × 49.5 cm)

Lady Cockburn and her Three Eldest Sons

Three boys cling to their mother in *Lady Cockburn and her Three Eldest Sons*, by Sir Joshua Reynolds. The mother and child theme is extended to form a whole family group. Use your finger to trace the rhythms their hands, arms and legs create. Does Reynolds successfully use these to link all four figures together. Describe the kinds of shapes your fingers has just traced. Do the four figures similarly link together if you allow the gaze of each to lead you from one to the other? Do all four figures look as if they belong together as a close knit family? They are obviously wealthy and consider themselves important. Think about the careers the boys will pursue when they grow up. Why do you think a parrot is included?

As in Campin's painting, your eye is eventually led to a distant view. Which of these views do you prefer and why? Draperies play a very important part in the design of this picture. They repeat the rhythms made by the family. Consider whether the scene is set in the artist's studio or in the home of the Cockburns. Imagine the kind of home the Cockburns would own. Would festoons of drapery normally hang around like this, or has the artist added them for effect? Do they enhance the overall effect of the painting or do you find them too contrived and artificial? Do you think wealthy families like the Cockburns will be pleased by Reynolds' approaches, and will regularly commission him?

If you have a younger brother or sister, make studies of them with a parent or guardian. Focus on special moments like storytime in the evening, when the closeness between the two is likely to be most apparent.

As well as responding to psychological relationships, try to formally link them, as Reynolds does. Get into the habit of observing the emotional and physical relationships that link parents and children when they are together in public places, as well as at home. Make studies of family groups, paying special attention to the kinds of rhythms and formal relationships that connect them. The psychological bonding between a parent and baby is usually apparent, but look, too at the body language of older children and their parents for clues to their relationships. Can loving relationships sometimes show strain as adolescents become conscious of their own identities and resentful of being treated like children? Think about how you can most effectively capture these nuances of interpersonal relationships.

Sir Joshua Reynolds, English (1723–1792)
Lady Cockburn and her Three Eldest Sons (1773)
Oil on Canvas
(141.6 × 113 cm)

A Family Group in a Landscape

Ten family members pose together in Frans Hals' *A Family Group in a Landscape*. Which are the parents? Do you think two or more generations are represented in this painting? Who do you think the woman holding the baby is on the right? Think about why families were usually bigger in the past than is generally the case today.

Allow your eye to revolve round this group, moving from one figure to another until you have taken account of all ten.

- Does Hals succeed in linking ten figures together as effectively as Reynolds manages to link four in his painting?

- Look at how Hals has linked them. Do some people command more attention than others, or are they all of equal interest?

- Are you conscious of any family resemblances? At least one hand of each person shows. Study all the hands, and then compare one with another. Is there any undue repetition or are they all in different positions?

- Now do the same with all ten heads. Take account of how upright or tilted each one is as well as considering the angle from which it is shown. Is there any repetition, or is each head unique formally and in its individuality and character? Does each hand look as if it is that of the person to whom it belongs? How would you describe the overall shape that the ten figures make?

The group is posed outside and, as in the previous two examples, sooner or later the eye moves to the distant view. Is this in keeping with the mood and tone of the family group? A distinctive glow illuminates the sky. Is this the light source creating the play of light and shade on each portrait head, and the colour scheme of the whole family group? When this was painted, many Dutch artists specialised in a particular genre of painting. Some, like Hals, were experts in portraiture, others in landscape, or still life. It is thought that the landscape view in *A Family Group in a Landscape* was painted by another artist rather than by Hals himself. What is your view of artists combining their talents in the same work in this kind of way? You may think it is practical, sensible and effective, or it may offend you if you feel that every work of art should be a unique expression of an individual artist's thoughts, feelings and ability.

Frans Hals, Dutch (about 1580(?)–1666)
A Family Group in a Landscape
(about 1647–50)
Oil on Canvas (148.5 × 251 cm)

Imagine you are at a wedding or a sporting occasion, and bride, groom and guests, or a team are posing for a group photograph. You are also recording the event, but must do so from an angle, because only the official photographer is allowed to stand in front of them. Produce a painting based on how the group is shortly before everybody poses officially. Will some people be laughing? Is there a joker in the group? Will people be sitting apart, or will some be holding hands or putting their arms round other people's shoulders? What eye contact will there be between one person and another?

How might you most effectively encourage the viewer's eye to move from one person to another in an interesting and varied way. Try to achieve sufficient uniformity between the various people to indicate that they are preparing for a group portrait, but bring interest into your composition by thinking about the different kinds of body language and the variations in the poses, positions, and attitudes of the various people involved. Some figures might have their arms folded, others clasping their hands, and so forth. Children can obviously bring contrasts in scale into the wedding version, but sports teams also frequently have young mascots. Consider what the setting is for this event, and decide where the light is coming from, how this will affect the play of light and shade, and the mood it will create.

The Virgin and Child with St Anne and St John the Baptist

Three generations are represented in this picture by Leonardo da Vinci. Find out why it is also known as *The Leonardo Cartoon*. Unlike the previous works considered, it is a drawing. Drawing is important to Degas' pastel paintings, but this charcoal and white chalk study is a drawing in its own right. You doubtless think of cartoons as animated films or comic strips. The *Leonardo Cartoon* clearly does not fit this definition. In what sense is it a cartoon? The word originally derives from an Italian word, *cartone*, meaning a large sheet of paper. A design for a fresco or panel painting was made, actual size, on this paper. Holes were then pricked into the outlines and charcoal dusted through to transfer the outline onto the painting surface. This might have been the intention when the cartoon was begun, but, as there are no prick marks on it, it seems likely that Leonardo continued to work on it, regarding it as a work of art in its own right.

Renaissance artists often arranged their figures within geometric shapes. Did Leonardo give unity to his figures by making them fit into such a shape? Can you also trace any rhythmic relationships Leonardo used to link them together? Did Leonardo use these to emphasise relationships between the figures together in the same way that Reynolds used them to link the various members of the Cockburn family? Do you sense any emotional links that might be connecting the four figures to each other?

Leonardo da Vinci, Italian (1452–1519)
The Virgin and Child with Saint Anne and Saint John the Baptist
(perhaps about 1499–1500)
Charcoal, black and white chalk on tinted paper (141.5 × 104.6 cm)

It is very fragile and, to prevent fading, hangs in a dimly lit room of its own in the National Gallery. If you have not yet been to the National Gallery, try to imagine yourself alone in this room, with all your attention focused on the Cartoon. In such a subdued atmosphere, it is like peering at an ancient altarpiece. And what exactly are you looking at? In the top right corner, there is the merest hint of landscape, and pebbles are suggested on the foreground floor. You are unlikely to even notice these for a while, though, for the composition, consisting of two women and two children, is completely dominated by the human figure.

Mr and Mrs Andrews

Thomas Gainsborough, English (1727–1788)
Mr and Mrs Andrews
(about 1748/9)
Oil on Canvas (69.8 × 119.4 cm)

Imagine you know Mr and Mrs Andrews. What do you think of them? How old are they and what are they like? Are they a sensible and likeable down-to-earth couple, or are they stuck-up, superior and full of fancy airs and graces? Are they close to each other, or do they have different interests, with each doing their own thing?

Do you think it is easier or more difficult to compose a picture of two people as opposed to groups of people or one person? Are you surprised by the position the couple occupy in this painting?

Gainsborough placed them on the extreme left of the canvas perhaps because he really wanted to paint landscapes but could not afford to do so. Or it may have been because Mr Andrews was a wealthy landowner and liked the idea of his whole estate, as well as his wife, being included to emphasise his status and importance. It is interesting to consider whether Mr and Mrs Andrews or Gainsborough himself derived most satisfaction from this painting.

Gainsborough painted a recently-married couple in *The Portrait of Mr and Mrs Andrews*, complete with a gun and dog to emphasise Mr Andrews' lifestyle and status. What does Mrs Andrews' pose and dress tell you about her? Do you think Gainsborough enjoyed painting the textures of rich, expensive materials? A bare patch of canvas remains where he obviously intended to paint something in her lap: try to imagine what she should be holding if this object had been painted in? Perhaps it would have been something Mrs Andrews loves and treasures, or something Mr Andrews had recently shot and killed.

The landscape in *Mr and Mrs Andrews* suggests that Gainsborough was a careful observer of the natural world and the effects of nature. To aid his later landscapes painted in his London studio, he created miniature versions, using mosses, lichens and clumps of foliage. He used coal to represent rocks, slivers of mirror for running water, and a stick of broccoli as a distant copse of trees. In this way, he formed special environments of his own – but **Environments** provides the theme of the next chapter.

Natural and Made

Around the Home

Environments is a Universal Theme in the most literal sense. It includes our immediate surroundings and the most distant places in this world and even beyond. We all live, work and play out our lives in environments. We sometimes find refreshment by changing one environment for another, by going on holiday, for example. We often feel nostalgic when we are away for too long, though. Think about your 'normal' environment and consider which of the places you have visited contrasts most strongly with it. Perhaps your bedroom comes to mind first, as this is probably the space over which you have most control.

Van Gogh's Chair

Van Gogh painted his bedroom at Arles several times. Its simple furniture includes two chairs. Just one of these provides the subject for *Van Gogh's Chair*. Though deceptively simple in terms of subject matter, the painting is complex in its content and meaning.

When are you most alive and alert, and work your best? What is your preferred stimulus and methods of working? Think about which things symbolise you in the way van Gogh and Gauguin's chairs symbolise them and choose an object that you think most effectively represents you and your interests. What colour scheme would do justice to both you and to it? What supporting objects could convey further information about you, your interests and concerns?

Make a painting or collage that aims to do justice to the chosen object but which also tells the viewer something about you and your temperament and personality.

Vincent van Gogh, Dutch (1853–1890)
Van Gogh's Chair (1888)
Oil on Canvas (91.8 × 73 cm)

Can you recall any other paintings consisting of just one simple object? It is of, 'just a single wooden, straw-coloured chair, yellow all over, standing on red tiles against a wall. Daylight'. The floor tiles tilt upwards in **Japanese perspective** (see page 66, 86). What does van Gogh mean by **Japanese perspective**? A box behind the chair contains sprouting bulbs. On the box is his signature, 'Vincent', and on the chair's rush seat are his pipe and tobacco pouch. This 'portrait' of a humble, ordinary chair has a presence and dignity of a sort more often associated with portraits of people. It is about van Gogh himself, as much as it is about a chair.

A companion painting in Amsterdam is of Gauguin's armchair. It is equally about him. Both paintings were begun in December 1888, when Gauguin was living and working with van Gogh in the south of France. Their regular quarrels contributed to van Gogh's breakdown later that month. Gauguin left, and to van Gogh the armchair became Gauguin's 'empty place'. In the painting, he seeks a 'red and green night effect' and places 'on the seat two novels and a candle'. Gauguin has an armchair, van Gogh a much more basic chair without arms. Consider what this tells us about the relationship between the two men. Which artist appears to thrive best in daylight and the sun, and prefers to work directly from nature? Which one seems to come to life after dark, finding his inspiration in books and literature?

A Young Woman Standing at a Virginal

Set in a typical Dutch 17th century interior, Vermeer's picture shows a young woman centrally placed against the back wall. Light catches the side of her face as she looks towards you. Her hands are on the keys of a virginal, which is an early kind of piano. Think about where the daylight is coming from to illuminate the scene.

A subtle play of light and shade is characteristic of Vermeer's work, and is an important element in his art. He consistently uses it to create a sense of space in his interiors. How would you describe the mood of this painting? Is anything happening, or is it a study in stillness?

What words would you use to describe the quality of the light? Note the subtle modulations of tone Vermeer achieves in the triangular shadow on the wall below the window level.

In the 20th century, another Dutch artist, Mondrian, painted abstract pictures composed of rectangular shapes. Is there a similar sense of (underlying) geometry in the repeated rectangular shapes of A Young Woman Standing at a Virginal? *Look at the framed pictures on the wall and on the upright lid of the virginal. Do you feel Vermeer attaches importance to their subject matter, or is he concerned only with the formal shapes they make?*

Jan Vermeer, Dutch (1632–1675)
A Young Woman Standing at a Virginal
(c.1670)
Oil on Canvas (51.7 × 45.2 cm)

Vermeer worked in Holland at a time when people other than the rich wanted to hang paintings in their homes. Consider what effect this might have had on the content and size of paintings compared with those commissioned by the church, or heads of state and aristocracy living in spacious palaces. Most of the resulting subject matter in Dutch art reflects the everyday lives and surroundings of people living in modest houses. Many 17th century Dutch paintings of this period closely relate to what you can still see in and around your own homes today.

The Courtyard of a House in Delft

The Courtyard of a House in Delft, by Pieter de Hooch, is about the beautiful counterplay between interior and outside views. The silhouetted back of the woman within contrasts with the woman and child, holding hands and chatting together, outside in the daylight walking towards you. Compare the dress of the woman with the child with that worn by the woman in the Vermeer, and think about the occupation and status of each woman.

Look closely at the interior section in de Hooch's painting. Cover up the surrounding areas so you can focus on it fully. Do you think it makes an interesting scene in its own right? Do the rosy bricks and creamy stones that surround the doorway seem to naturally frame this view? De Hooch is famous for the ways in which he creates pictures within pictures like this.

Using the theme 'Inside and Outside' as your starting point, discover compositions in and around your home that form pictures within pictures. Using windows or doorways to look out from inside, or in from outside, find viewpoints that include both aspects.

- *How does the light within compare with that outside?*

- *Do any interior shapes relate to those outside?*

- *How might you use these to achieve greater unity in your work?*

- *Are there interesting contrasts between the two worth emphasising?*

De Hooch composes in a range of warm ochres and rosy reds. Study the colour schemes which characterise your home and the immediate surroundings. Using your observations as a basis, produce a painting or collage that combines interior and exterior views of your home, and reflects its character and mood.

Pieter de Hooch, Dutch (1629–1684)
The Courtyard of a House in Delft (1658)
Oil on Canvas (73.5 × 60 cm)

A Woman and her Maid in a Courtyard

In *A Woman and her Maid in a Courtyard*, de Hooch creates a composition out of the kind of brick floor, outbuildings and immediate surroundings you might see outside your own back door. The chimneys and rooftops of neighbouring houses break the skyline, as do the branches of a leafless tree. Through a half-open gate, you can see a man approaching. Who do you think he is? A woman, who may be the lady of the house, has her back to us and hand outstretched, while she speaks to a maid. The maid kneels, conveniently close to an outside tap and sink, cleaning and preparing fish for the evening meal. De Hooch precisely observes the nearby bowl, bucket and broom, its handle against the wall, creating a distinctive foreground still-life group. Is this another example of a picture within a picture? Look carefully at the uneven brick paving of the courtyard in the foreground. Do you agree with Gordon's observation that de Hooch paints these so convincingly that 'it seems as if the picture's very surface is buckling'?

What confronts you when you step outside your back door? Do you step onto a path, patio or paved area? Are there any objects like buckets or gardening tools around? Is there a garden or lawn? Are you aware of other buildings beyond, or do natural features like trees and fields dominate?

Consider whether these views look more or less interesting from upstairs or downstairs windows. Try to find foreground features to use as framing devices, or to emphasise the contrast between near and far. Think about how these views vary at different times of the day or even throughout the year. As well as recording them in your sketchbook, photograph them if you can.

Try to build up a comprehensive picture of your home, the immediate surroundings, and the relationships that connect the two.

Pieter de Hooch, Dutch (1629–1684)
A Woman and her Maid in a Courtyard (c.1660/1)
Oil on Canvas (73.7 × 62.6 cm)

People have always reshaped and altered their environments to meet a wide variety of needs. Eileen Adams and John Ward believe that 'Churches, factories, houses, institutions, palaces, schools, fortresses, buildings of all kinds and their relationship to each other; monuments, statues, and all kinds of urban paraphenalia; open spaces and waste spaces – all of these combine to make a setting for the human drama played out in the urban theatre we have created for ourselves.' The urban landscape is obviously shaped by people, but we often think of rural surroundings as natural – even down to small clusters of buildings nestling snugly amongst trees. In reality, the layout of fields, walls and hedges, woodland areas and waterways that characterise many a rural scene are just as likely to be structured and organised by people. What is your local environment like?

The Avenue at Middelharnis

In *The Avenue at Middelharnis*, Hobbema vividly communicates the feeling of being in the middle of a journey. Do you sense this? Think about what features in the painting contribute to this feeling. The likely destination seems to be the village in the distance. Are you, therefore, midway between one village and the next? The tall trees dominate the painting. They plunge towards the village in dramatic perspective, diminishing in scale as they recede. Examine how Hobbema ensured sufficient variety in the trees to avoid monotony. They are so tall they dwarf the people in the landscape. In what tasks are these various people engaged?

What is your journey from home to school or college like? Do you walk, cycle, go by car, bus or train? Is it a rural or urban journey or a mixture of the two? Is it all much of a muchness or does it vary from one part to another? Think about any significant buildings or landmarks and whether any mark the way, or are sufficiently interesting for you to look forward to seeing them. Close your eyes and retrace your journey in your mind's eye. Do you see it from any particular point?

Make a painting, collage, 3-D assemblage or ceramic panel to sum up your journey from home to school. What shapes, forms and colours best characterise your journey? Make sketches and take photographs of significant features so you can incorporate them in your work. Hobbema records his view by looking straight down the road as if he is standing in the middle of it.

Meindert Hobbema, Dutch (1638–1709)
The Avenue at Middelharnis (1689)
Oil on Canvas
(103.5 × 141 cm)

Bush Potato Dreaming

Look closely at *Bush Potato Dreaming*. The symbols Aboriginal artists use can have different meanings which may lead to a variety of interpretations. Imagine you are looking down onto a desert landscape from above. The black horseshoe shapes usually indicate people. What do you think the lines and circles are most likely to indicate in a desert context? In addition to surface landmarks, like waterholes and dreamtime journey lines, Aboriginal artists sometimes also refer to underground passageways, chambers and water sources, as if they can see the landscape through X-ray eyes. Could some of the lines in 'Bush Potato Dreaming' show where potatoes are below the surface?

Traditional Aboriginal paintings are on tree bark and are black, white, yellow ochre and red ochre paint, made out of earth and other natural pigments. This painting, like many now being produced, is in acrylic paint on canvas. Even though acrylic paints in tubes encourage the use of a wide range of colours, many modern Aboriginal artists deliberately choose to remain faithful to their four colour tradition. These colours have come to symbolise the Australian bush and its people.

Do any particular colours and tones come to mind when you reflect on the environment through which you pass on your journey from home to school?

To capture the essence of your journey, you might choose to represent it in plan form, as if seen from above. To help you do this, see what your journey looks like by tracing it on a detailed map of the area. In representing their Dreamtime Walkabouts, Aboriginal artists often represent the land as if they are looking down on it from above.

Bush Potato Dreaming, Yuendumu, NT Australia (1986)
Acrylic on canvas (145 × 94 cm)
Courtesy of the Trustees of the British Museum

The Interior of the Grote Kerk at Haarlem

Think of particular buildings you sometimes enter and so know from
the inside, such as a favourite shop or place of worship. Saenredam
specialised in church interiors, like *The Grote Kerk at Haarlem*. The
colour scheme is unusual and very distinctive. Think about what it
consists of. It has been described as a kind of symphony in white. Is
there more than one source of light in *The Grote Kerk*? The play of
light helps create warmer notes of colour here and there, and the artist
successfully uses areas of shadow to suggest three dimensional form.

Pieter Saenredam, Dutch (1597–1665)
The Interior of the Grote Kerk at Haarlem
(1636–7)
Oil on Oak (59.5 × 81.7 cm)

What is the interior of your local church like? Is it light or
dark? Where does the light come from? If it has clerestory
windows, what kind of light effects do they create as the
light slants downwards from above? Are there stained
glass windows? Do these create unusual coloured light
effects when sunlight shines through them? Is it a gloomy
environment, reliant on artificial light for most of the
time?

Make studies of your local church interior, taking account
of its particular lighting effects. What colour are the
walls? Examine the problems of colour mixing and use of
tone that Saenredam must have overcome in painting an
all-white interior. Perhaps your church has white walls.

In order to help you deal with the problems an interior
like this poses, try setting up and painting a still-life group
consisting only of white objects – for example a bottle of
milk, eggs on a plate, a white jug and draperies. Can you
create the form and shape of each object in space, and
record the tonal range of each object by carefully
observing the play of light and shade on it?

Consider whether the virtual absence of colour, other than white, makes creating space in a painting easier or more difficult. A few black diamond shapes do appear, but most of the picture area shows the characteristic whitewashed walls so typical of sober Dutch Protestant churches.

The Stonemason's Yard

Giovanni Antonio Canal, called Canaletto, Italian (1697–1768)
*Venice: Campo S. Vidal and S. Maria della Carità
(The Stonemason's Yard) 1726–30*
Oil on Canvas (123.8 × 162.9 cm)

Light and shade is crucial to The Stonemason's Yard. *Langmuir observes that the 'Thundery clouds are gradually clearing, and the sun casts powerful shadows, whose steep diagonals help define the space and articulate the architecture'. Half close your eyes so that you become less aware of colour values and more conscious of broad tonal areas. Does this help make you more aware of major areas of light and dark tone and less aware of objects? Make a diagram of the main blocks of light and dark tone that make up the design of this painting. Canaletto paints on top of a reddish brown ground rather than the white one he usually preferred. Think about whether or not this contributes* to the rich tonality of The Stonemason's Yard. *Instead of taking account of only the more familiar views you might choose for a postcard, explore the less obvious, less attractive aspects of your surroundings. Observe how the familiar can seem quite different and even strange when seen from unexpected angles or viewpoints. Use your sketchbook to record your environment from viewpoints you find interesting, but which will not be necessarily immediately recognisable to friends and neighbours. Turn prevailing weather conditions to advantage, noting how these can 'help define space and articulate the architecture', just as Canaletto used passing storm effects.*

Do you ever take a short cut on your way to school? Perhaps this takes you across waste ground or behind buildings you usually see from the front. Have you noticed how, when on a train, you often see unfamiliar aspects of a city or townscape as you travel past back gardens, and the backs of factories and warehouses? These routes highlight views the popular tourist itineraries take great care to avoid. The Venetian artist Canaletto, more than any other, painted typical Venetian views to appeal to the tastes of those on the 18th century Grand Tours – views still offered to tourists by the postcard trade today. Though Canaletto is closely associated with these fashionable views, he sometimes painted the less familiar.

The Stonemason's Yard is an untypical back view of the kind you might see from a train window. Is this scene viewed from ground level or from a higher vantage point? Where do you think Canaletto might have positioned himself in order to see it? Bright sunlight vividly illuminates the large lumps of stone in the foreground. Others are lost in deep shadow. A workman cuts stone by a wooden building that looks quite temporary. A woman attempting to control her children, is observed by another woman hanging out of an upstairs window. The church across the canal is in strong shadow, its bell tower silhouetted against the sky.

The Elements

Built environments will always be subject to the ravages of time, the seasons and the elements, whatever we may try to do to prevent this. Fire, tempest and earthquake can destroy the most permanently conceived buildings and monuments. Nature's power is impressive. In our ever-diminishing world, we still retain a basic impulse to periodically escape, to feel free and experience the wonder of wild and natural places that are still untouched and untamed.

Adam Elsheimer, German (1578–1610)
Saint Paul on Malta (c.1600)
Oil on Copper (16.8 × 21.3 cm)

Saint Jerome in a Rocky Landscape

A monastery and other buildings appear in *Saint Jerome in a Rocky Landscape*, but the painting still reveals Patenier's interest in wild, untamed places. To what extent do you think the dark, inky tone of the sky determines the overall mood of this painting? To what extent is it determined by the strangeness of the landscape? Have you ever been to or seen anywhere similar?

Patenier was Netherlandish. Many Northern European artists travelled to Italy to study its art at that time. Think about how they would have travelled and how long the journey might be. Some were as impressed by the Alps themselves as by the art of Italy. Why would rocky, mountainous landscapes seem so impressive to Dutch and Flemish travellers?

Little is known about Patenier's life. Do you think the painting indicates he has actually seen mountains like these, that travellers' tales have caught his imagination or that he simply invents them?

Attributed to: Joachim Patenier, Netherlandish (active 1515, died no later than 1524)
Saint Jerome in a Rocky Landscape
(probably 1515–24)
Oil on Oak (36.2 × 34.3 cm)

Landscape with a Ruined Castle and a Church

How much of Ruisdael's painting is devoted to sky? Compared with other landscapes you have studied, does its low horizon make it seem unconventional? Is the sky interesting enough to justify it occupying such an expanse of canvas?

Find locations which give you a clear view of the horizon, and make a series of studies in which sky fills most of the picture area. Visit these places on days when the cloud effects make the sky particularly interesting, with a view to increasing your awareness of cloud and sky effects, and your skills in representing them.

Jacob van Ruisdael, Dutch (1628/9?–1682)
A Landscape with a Ruined Castle and a Church
(c.1665–70)
Oil on Canvas
(109 × 146 cm)

Landscape with a Ruined Castle and a Church, by Ruisdael shows a typical Low Countries environment. What a contrast to the scenes Patenier preferred to paint! Does Ruisdael succeed in adding interest to these flat surroundings? Compare his landscape with Canaletto's *The Stonemason's Yard*, and consider which is most dramatic in its use of tonal contrasts.

To Infinity – and Beyond

The earliest works in the National Gallery were painted at a time when people still believed the world was flat. The collection extends up to the 20th century, during which moon walks and space exploration has taken place. At this very minute, spaceships are circling planets millions of miles away, increasing our knowledge of environments in deepest space. People have gazed at the stars for centuries, and contemplated the infinite. 'But the sight of the stars always sets me dreaming just as naively as those black dots on the map set me dreaming of towns and villages. Why should those points of light in the firmament, I wonder, be less accessible than the dark ones on the map', wrote van Gogh to his brother Theo. Long before spaceships made space travel possible, people were able to visit these far-away places in their dreams and imaginations. Their existence is explained in countless stories and myths.

The Origin of the Milky Way

The painting's title tells you what it is about. How much of the story of how the Milky Way was created can you reconstruct from the clues to be found within the painting? It actually shows the infant Hercules rousing the goddess Juno. The milk from her breasts turns into the stars of the Milky Way. Unfortunately, the lower part of the painting was cut off long ago, so the lilies created by the milk as it touches the ground are no longer visible. Do you think Tintoretto and his contemporaries literally believed these ancient myths?

Jacopo Tintoretto, Italian (1518–1594)
The Origin of the Milky Way
(probably 1575–80)
Oil on Canvas
148 × 165.1 cm)

Tintoretto's *The Origin of the Milky Way* illustrates an ancient Greek creation myth. Far more is known about the Milky Way now, and how stars form, than was the case then, over 400 years ago. Ironically, though, we are now less aware of the Milky Way than people were then. Brightly lit towns and cities light up the immediate surroundings, but make it virtually impossible to see star galaxies as Tintoretto and his contemporaries could clearly see them on any clear night.

Tintoretto uses foreshortening to present the story in a vividly dramatic way. The figures sweep energetically around in space. In order to stimulate his imagination to depict scenes like this, Tintoretto made small wax figures and arranged them with architectural models or hung them from the ceiling as if they were flying overhead. He experimented with lighting to heighten the dramatic effects, and then recorded the figures by making rapid charcoal drawings of them.

Finding the Infinite in Ordinary Places

Monet's *Water-Lilies* was certainly one of the most popular paintings in the National Gallery prior to its transfer to the Tate in March 1997. Having created his own garden pond, Monet represents it over and over again. Robert Hughes says, 'The pond was a slice of infinity', but what does he mean? Instead of looking into the sky and dreaming, Monet finds infinity by studying a small patch of water. Stand quietly in front of the painting for a while. Move towards it, allowing it to completely fill your field of vision. What words most effectively describe the feelings and sensations you experience as you allow the mood of *Water-Lilies* to exert its spell on you?

Water-Lilies

There is no horizon, and little sense of foreground or background, in this painting. Do you nevertheless consider it to be a landscape? The brushstrokes form surface marks, but also suggest depth. When you focus your attention on the surface, are you looking at the surfaces of the water, of the picture or both?

Some areas indicate depth. Can you sense other layers between the surface and the greatest depth? What time of day is it and what is the weather like? Is *Water-Lilies* simply a painting of water, reflected sky and flowers, or is it about more and if so, what?

Imagine you are Claude Monet peering into his pond, paintbrush in hand. What sorts of sensations are you experiencing and what can you actually see? Does the painting successfully capture all these kinds of sensations? Large numbers of reproductions of *Water-Lilies* are sold each year. Assuming most are purchased by visitors who like the painting, what is there about it that makes so many people so responsive to it?

You could experiment with the idea of subject matter filling the whole picture area and extending beyond its boundaries. Study wall surfaces. Make sketches and take photographs, focusing on the colours, shapes, textures and layerings you can find within them. Take account of weathering, crumbling surfaces suggestive of age and indicating depth. Wood, brick, plaster and stone might have been applied to the surface at different times, reappearing now as the top surfaces crumble away.

Some surfaces might show graffiti, or the remnants of posters once stuck on them. Others might have been painted many times over, with weathering creating areas of colour and texture which now resurface. Interior walls of part-demolished houses, exposed to the elements, might similarly reveal layers of long-forgotten wallpaper.

Using your observations, your sketches and photographs as the basis, produce an art work in which the wall surface fills the whole picture area. The subject is an ideal one for the combined use of materials like collage, paint, 'found' and assemblage materials. Which combinations of colour and texture, pattern and shape, layering, blurring, and use of sharp focus will enable you to most potently convey infinity through the subject of walls?

Reassurance in the Familiar

Landscape views are arguably the paintings which appeal most directly to popular taste today. Their very popularity can cause you to take them for granted, and almost disregard them. You think you know what they look like, so do not bother to look at them any more.

The Hay-Wain

You will already be familiar with *The Hay-Wain* by Constable. Everybody has seen it reproduced in some form or other. It is probably the most familiar landscape painting in the country.

Try to recall where and when you first saw it, and how it was reproduced. It may have been on a plate, table mat, tray top, or chocolate box lid, or on the wall of a holiday hotel you once stayed in, perhaps. Does a reproduction of it hang in your own home? You might even have a jigsaw puzzle of it, for it is reproduced in every conceivable way. All this merchandising makes it quite difficult to look at *The Hay-Wain* with a fresh eye.

Examine its overall effect from a distance, therefore, and then study it closely in detail, and consider whether there is anything there to account for its widespread appeal? The weather is important. Scudding clouds cross the sky, causing a fitful play of sunlight on the fields and foliage. Is it going to rain? We know what time of day it is – the original title was *Landscape, Noon*. What time of year is it, though? Contemplate the feeling of being in the hay-wain, crossing the water on a day like this, and try to remember experiencing fresh air, the sun's warmth, and a gentle breeze on your face in a similar setting. Do you think Constable successfully captured a mood many people already associate with warm summer days when a sudden shower might occur, in a typically English rural setting?

Study the foliage of the trees in *The Hay-Wain*. Why are there white flecks and speckles in the green? Unkind critics labelled these, 'Constable's snow', but think about why he added them. Perhaps it was to break up what might otherwise be monotonous areas of green, or to suggest the shimmer of a breeze that constantly reveals the pale reverse sides of the leaves. The horses' harnesses are red. Similar small notes of red occur in virtually all Constable's landscape paintings. Red is the complementary colour to green, being warm in colour whereas green is cool. Why do you think these notes of red are introduced into an otherwise predominantly green landscape?

Do you think *The Hay-Wain* is of an actual place Constable knew? Does it look as if it was based on direct observation, preliminary studies, his memory, imagination, or a combination of these? The scene is of a view of Flatford Mill, which was owned by his father, a miller. Situated close to the Suffolk and Essex border, it is not in a spectacular area, like the Lake District or the Cornish coast, but Constable's paintings ensure it is now a popular tourist attraction.

Constable never tired of recording this area in sketchbooks as well as in small 'on-the-spot' oil and watercolour studies.

John Constable, English (1776–1837)
The Hay-Wain (1821)
Oil on Canvas (130.2 × 185.4 cm)

If growing up in a rural environment made Constable a painter, what can your locality offer you? Does it stimulate your interest, or do you find it frankly dull and boring? Is it claustrophobic or is it characterised by open spaces revealing distant vistas? Make a series of studies that take full account of the near and far, the small-scale and the large. Note which main features and landmarks typify the place, and the balance between its natural and built components.

How colourful or monochromatic a place is it? Consider which colours are most representative of its mood, and which ones most effectively express your feelings about the place and its atmosphere.

Using sketchbooks and an appropriate variety of media, build up a visual record of your locality over an extended period of time. Identify a number of key vantage points and explore the compositional possibilities these present. Constable preferred to represent his landscapes in a midday light. What weather conditions and times of day present the best opportunities for you to express what you want to say about the area you live in? Work in varying weather conditions and at different times of the day to enable you to become more sensitive to the range of moods and atmospheres your locality offers. Which are most suited to your needs?

He painted many freely and rapidly, enabling him to capture momentary light effects and transient moods of nature. The area so stimulated his senses, he painted it over and over again throughout his life, and wrote 'the sound of water escaping from Mill dams, willows, old rotten planks, slimy posts and brick-work – I love such things. These scenes made me a painter, and I am grateful.'

Extremes: Nature versus the Industrial Revolution

Compare *The Hay-Wain* with *The Fighting 'Temeraire'*, painted by Turner, a contemporary of Constable. These oil paintings vie with each other for popularity today. Look at the two paintings. Think about what the differences tell you about the artists' characters. Compare their approaches to nature and the elements. Constable preferred to study a small corner of England in the light of day. Turner loved the extremes of nature – mountain ranges, ravines, blizzards, storms at sea and, in particular, dramatic sunrises and sunsets. In pursuit of these, he tirelessly travelled all over Britain and Europe, seeking out dramatic and spectacular places.

The Fighting 'Temeraire'

The sunset in *The Fighting 'Temeraire'* is particularly eye-catching. It commands your attention straightaway, but what do you notice once you allow your eye to move to the sky and water to the left of the ship? Focus specifically on this section, and examine how the colour and mood in this area contrasts with that of the sunset. How does it relate to your first impression of the overall colour, impact and mood of the painting? The smooth surface of the calm water acts like a reflective mirror. Do the colours and tones in this expanse of water significantly affect the mood of the painting? Cover up as much of the water as you can, and see whether this alters your feelings towards the work as a whole.

Turner witnessed the beginnings of the Industrial Revolution and the development of steam power. The full title of this painting is *The Fighting 'Temeraire' tugged to her last berth to be broken up, 1838*. The 'Temeraire', was a famous battleship, and distinguished herself at the Battle of Trafalgar. This is her last journey. Do you think Turner expresses sympathy for this ship, either in the actual treatment of the ship or through the painting as a whole? Look at how he contrasts the tug with the sailing ship it pulls, and consider whether he also has nostalgic feelings towards the tug. On the evidence of this painting, where do you feel Turner's preferences lie, with the passing era of sail or the dawning age of steam?

Study the painting and consider whether Turner actually saw the 'Temeraire' being towed along the Thames to be broken up at Rotherhithe. Does it look like a literal representation of an event he witnessed? Turner may have adapted an observed or reported event, idealising and enhancing the subject matter in the process. The painting shows the final voyage of an important ship. Think about why Turner chose to show it at late evening, set against a magnificent sunset and with a crescent moon in the sky. According to anecdote, Turner saw the 'Temeraire' being towed to the breaker's yard. In fact, all its masts had already been removed, and Turner was abroad at the time, so did not see the event. Do you think Turner's imaginative recreation of the event does adequate justice to the memory of a noble ship?

Like Constable, Turner made countless sketches and watercolour studies directly from nature, and brilliant skies feature prominently in them.

Vivid sunrises and sunsets arouse in most people a sense of wonder and awe, of the sublime and the infinite. Are you able to observe either sunrises or sunsets from your bedroom window, or do you have to go outside to observe them?

Using watercolours and pastels, record the many variations to be observed in sunrises and sunsets. You will doubtless want to record the range and variety of colour. However, in order to avoid crudity, take care to compose within a colour scheme. What is your favourite outdoor subject matter? Use your sunrise and sunset studies to further imbue these subjects with atmospheric qualities and mood and, perhaps, added meaning. You may want to experiment with extreme lighting conditions to formally explore your subject matter.

Joseph Mallord William Turner, English
(1775–1851)
*Rain, Steam and Speed – The Great Western
Railway*
(before 1844)
Oil on Canvas (90.8 × 121.9 cm)

Turner communicates a vivid feeling of speed in this painting. How does the speed of an 1844 train relate to our notions of speed today? Nowadays, people often object to road construction. What kind of impact did railway construction have on the environment then?

Running along the railway line ahead of the train is a hare. Think about why Turner included a hare and what symbolic significance it has. Perhaps it signifies the fear that rural England is being eroded by the relentless advance of the Industrial Revolution.

The train is crossing the River Thames over the Maidenhead Viaduct, designed by Brunel. What do you think the viaduct on the left would be for at that time? Does the painting make you think Turner is sympathetic to the new modes of transport? The train contrasts with the boats below. Is the shipping representative of more traditional modes of transport?

Make a 2-D or 3-D work in any medium or media to communicate late-20th century concepts of speed and transport. As preparation, gather sketchbook data about various modes of transport. If you aim to work three dimensionally, make a maquette so you can envisage the eventual piece more fully 'in the round'. Rotate it to ensure it looks pleasing from any angle. Consider the shapes, rhythms and forms that are most effective in suggesting speed and streamlining. Also gather relevant material from secondary sources. Use all this material and information to make your own late-20th century equivalent of Turner's statement about the speed, transport and technology of 1844, as epitomised by Rain, Steam and Speed.

Rain, Steam and Speed, is another famous Turner oil painting that relates directly to the Industrial Revolution. How does its mood compare with that of *The Fighting 'Temeraire'*? What time of day is it here? The title tells you it is raining – look at how Turner conveys this. We take trains for granted today. Imagine yourself growing up in 1844. Contemplate your reaction to these new steam trains and the construction of vast railway networks linking one end of the country to the other. Compare *Rain, Speed and Steam* with the *Avenue at Middelharnis* (page 45). The paintings are obviously dissimilar in mood and technique. Whereas Hobbema leads the eye into the picture through his use of perspective, Turner uses it to dramatically bring the eye forward. Does this increase the sensation of the train rushing towards you?

A strange feature of Turner's train is the firebox at the front of the engine. He uses 'artistic licence' for dramatic effect. Even at this early stage in the development of steam trains, coal had to be fed into the boiler from a footplate at the rear of the engine. The 'Rocket' is one of the most famous early steam trains. A painting of it on a pub sign shows its firebox being stoked at the rear of the engine. The sign also includes its designer: Who was he?

'The Rocket' pub sign, The Chat Moss Hotel, Glazebury, England

New Functions for Railway Architecture

The examples of Industrial Revolution railway architecture that survive are generally admired today. Some are being imaginatively adapted to new functions, giving them a new lease of life.

Providing an integrated transport system for Madrid has led to people boarding and alighting from trains before they enter the magnificent 19th century station. Instead of being demolished, it has been turned into an extraordinary tropical rainforest-like environment full of cafes, walkways, seating and, of course, humidity. Some of the plants now stand many metres high, their fronds dwarfing the people below.

Are there any buildings from this era close to where you live? What worthwhile functions, that would benefit the community, do you think they could fulfil if restored?

Atocha Railway Station, Madrid, Spain

Shifting Viewpoints

In the 19th century the desire to travel overland was matched by an equal desire to travel upwards. An early photographer, Nadar, went up in a balloon to photograph Paris in 1859. Have you ever looked down from a plane and felt surprise at how different everything looks? Have you seen photographs of the earth from space? Imagine you lived in Paris, prior to air and space travel. How would you react to Nadar's aerial views of Paris? The impact on some of the Impressionist painters living in and around Paris was to select high viewpoints from which to study the cityscape afresh. They set up their easels by upper storey windows to look down onto the boulevards below, full of scurrying people and horse drawn carriages.

The Boulevard Montmartre at Night

In *The Boulevard Montmartre at Night*, Camille Pissarro painted Paris by night. It shows one of the first artificially lit cityscapes like those we still see today when we go out at night. Can you tell from the painting whether the boulevard is illuminated by gas or by the new electric lighting? The Impressionists were among the first artists who could use oil paint in tubes. Earlier artists had to mix their paint as they needed it. It was difficult to do this outside the studio. The availability of paint in tubes contributed to a revolution. It enabled artists to leave their studios to set up their easels outside, if they chose. Consider how this might have influenced the size of Impressionist paintings and their choice of subject matter.

Think about whether working directly in front of the motif makes painting easier or more difficult, and what specific technical problems might arise. Does working in this manner affect how artists think, see and work? A critic-friend of the Impressionists, Gustave Geffroy, maintained, 'It is a question of houses in groups, crossing carriages, moving pedestrians. One has no time to see a man, a carriage, and the painter who lingers over detail will fail to catch the confusion of movements and the multiple spots which form the whole'. Examine how Pissarro painted individual figures, carriages and buildings.

In addition to its detail, consider the overall effect of the painting from a distance. Do the 'multiple spots' add up to form a unified whole? How successful is Pissarro as judged by Geffroy's criteria? Pissarro admits that the unity 'the human spirit gives to vision can only be found in the studio. It is there that our impressions, previously scattered, are co-ordinated and enhance each others' value'. Pissarro completed *The Boulevard Montmartre at Night* in the hotel room he was using as a studio. Do you think he might have started off looking carefully at the view from the window, and then concentrated on the painting itself in order to organise his impressions?

Paint the view from your bedroom window by night, bearing in mind Geffroy's advice about speed and detail. Use oil, acrylic, gouache or poster colour. Decide whether you want to work on a white or a coloured ground and prepare your painting surface accordingly.

Experiment with lighting to help you see what you are actually painting without your view 'washing out'. Observe the subject closely, and work as rapidly as you can without losing control. Keep the mood of the view and the overall effect you desire firmly in mind throughout. Is the colour and tonal range narrow or are there any strong contrasts?

Look at which colours predominate and do not linger over detail.

Approach the task as directly as you can, using a broad, free technique similar to that of Pissarro. To help you achieve the unity he sought, work in a more considered way later. Ensure, though, that you remain true to the mood and sensations experienced while in front of the actual view. Compare this painting with a similar nocturnal scene executed using more conventional approaches based on sketches and your memory.

Exotic Places of the Imagination

Pissarro painted his cityscape on a wet night. Look at which brushstrokes most effectively capture the feeling of wetness. Examine once more Turner's method of representing areas of swirling mist and rain in *Rain, Steam and Speed*, and consider how he achieved the effects he wanted. In addition to a paintbrush, is it possible he applies and smears the paint with his fingers and rags?

Tiger in a Tropical Storm (Surprised!)

Look at Rousseau's technique for showing sheeting tropical rain in *Tiger in a Tropical Storm (Surprised!)*. Compare it with Turner's complex variety of means. Rousseau used one simple, if unusual, device. It is not so apparent in reproductions, but when you visit the National Gallery, make sure you look closely at the streaks he added to the painting to indicate slanting rain. Do you think they successfully convey the effect of heavy rain falling?

Pissarro's painting is directly observed, at least in its initial stages. Both Turner's paintings are imaginative but could relate to actual experiences. It is unlikely that Rousseau ever saw a tiger in a tropical storm, as he never left France, so this scene is purely imaginary. In order to represent an event he has never experienced as authentically as he can, what do you think Rousseau did? How would you go about acquiring the essential information necessary for you to paint a scene like this, without actually going to the place itself?

The invention of heated greenhouses made it possible to grow magnificent tropical plants in places like London's Kew Gardens. Zoos and safari parks also provide access to tropical animals. Rousseau studied plants and animals in the Jardin des Plantes in Paris, for it contains both exotic plants and animals. In the foreground of his painting, you will probably recognise enlarged versions of familiar houseplants like 'mother-in-law's tongue'. It is, of course, equally possible to visit anywhere in your daydreams. Do you think Rousseau successfully uses his observations of plants and animals to make the exotic places he imagines, and loves to paint, more vivid and convincing?

Think about how a more imaginative work like *Tiger in a Tropical Storm (Surprised!)* differs from one more obviously based on direct observation, like *The Hay-Wain*. Rousseau is often referred to as a 'Sunday painter'. As a customs officer, with no formal art training he painted only in his spare time. This may have been reflected in the painting. The tiger is surprised. Do you think this is causing it to cower in fear, or to crouch ready to pounce? Does it look fearsome, or as tame as a kitten? Do his observations of plants enable him to convincingly paint tropical rainforests? Do any of these things matter? Is the world of Rousseau sufficiently charming for you to willingly suspend any sense of disbelief for whatever time you are able to spend in it?

Henri Rousseau, French (1844–1910)
Tiger in a Tropical Storm (Surprised!)
(1891)
Oil on Canvas (129.8 × 161.9 cm)

Make studies of cactus, tropical plants and animals by visiting glasshouses, garden centres, zoos, safari parks or museums with collections of stuffed animals and skeletons. You might find it helpful to substantiate what you do by studying the movements and anatomy of such domestic pets as cats and dogs. Use all the information you gather as the basis for an imaginative painting, collage or textile panel of a tropical or exotic place.

Emphasise the density of your environment by filling most of the picture area with bushes, trees and plants. You might also want to suggest depth through overlapping. To ensure your work is as decoratively rich as possible, introduce a range and variety of texture, pattern and colour. Repeat pattern shapes to give unity to your design, but also seek variety and contrast in the size and shapes of leaves, and in their veins and surface markings. You might add interest by allowing occasional glimpses of details of some of the animals, birds and reptiles that inhabit this place. Be inventive, as well as literal, in your choice of colour.

Persian Miniature

Whatever has surprised the tiger remains unseen. Everything is visible in a miniature from the Persian Book of Kings, though. Rustam lies asleep on a striped rug in a woody landscape. A lion is about to attack him. Fortunately, his horse is wide awake and alert, and saves him as he sleeps on, blissfully unaware. How does the horse attack the lion, and how is the lion reacting? Might the snake, slithering up a tree on the left, pose a further threat?

Make a comparison of the range of flora the artist includes, noting the wide variety of patterns and shapes they make, with the flora in Rousseau's landscape. Which artist do you feel shows most inventiveness in the treatment of flora? Which appears to possess the more extensive knowledge of botany? Which remains most faithful to the actual colours of foliage? Which is the more pleasing painting in terms of colour, pattern, decorative qualities, and atmosphere?

Allow your eye to roam over the Persian miniature, taking in its details one by one. Do you find it more natural to 'read' this painting from front to back, or from top to bottom?

What does the way objects overlap suggest to you? Some trees and plants are clearly behind the large, central tree, and therefore seem further away. Look at the lion's feet in relation to this tree. Does the base of the tree make the lion seem to be above ground level? What effect does the tree behind Rustam have?

Do details like this disturb you, or do you feel they do not matter in a painting that tells its story so vividly and is characterised by graceful rhythms, pattern, and a lyrical use of colour?

Rustam Asleep, Persian Book of Miniatures
From the Sháháma of Firdausi
Persia [Iran] (c.1470) Minature (31.6 × 20.8 cm)
Courtesy of the Trustees of the British Museum

Bathers at Asnières

Seurat was a Parisian contemporary of Rousseau. He died young, but produced a small number of important and influential paintings and a series of distinctive conté crayon drawings. *Bathers at Asnières* was painted seven years before Rousseau's tiger. The steaming humidity of a tropical storm is replaced by the lazy calm and stillness of a hot, cloudless summer day on the banks of the Seine. People relax on the grass. Is there any evidence of movement or activity in the painting?

Georges-Pierre Seurat, French (1859–1891)
Bathers at Asnières (1884)
Oil on Canvas (201 × 300 cm)

Seurat invented **pointillism**, a technique using small coloured dots of paint rather than conventional brushstrokes. The method relies on the eye optically 'mixing' the dots of colour as the viewer steps back from the canvas. In order to make a colour more pure and intense, Seurat surrounded it with its opposite. For example, blue is opposite to orange on the colour circle. It is as cool as orange is warm. Placed next to blue, orange looks much more intense than when it is surrounded by reds and yellows.

Impressionist experiments include using coloured frames to enhance the colour schemes of paintings. Seurat sometimes painted dots on his frames to complement colour in the adjacent area of painting. Try a small experiment of your own.

Collect paint samples from a home improvement store. Put four samples of the same red on a board. Surround one mainly with the greens, another with harmonising reds, the next with purples and blues, and the last with oranges and yellows. Does the red appear to change according to which colours surround it? If you did not know already, would you be surprised to discover they are all the same red?

If you look carefully at the shaded area of the orange hat, worn by the bathing boy, you will see some small blue and orange dots Seurat added later. Note how he also added some pale creamy dots to the water to the left of the boy.

Try to recall relaxing by water or on a grassy bank on a similar warm summer day, and consider whether Seurat successfully captured the kinds of sensations you associate with that experience.

Seurat is often described as a **Neo-Impressionist**, meaning that he modified Impressionism by using more formal approaches to composition and colour. The Impressionists painted their landscapes outside in front of the motif, often adding to them later in the studio. Consider whether this painting is much larger than a typical Impressionist canvas? Do you think Seurat started it outside, or painted it entirely in his studio? What leads you to your conclusion? Do you think Seurat painted it rapidly, or constructed it patiently and methodically? Think about whether the scene is directly observed, or based on preliminary drawn and painted studies. Estimate the timescale from when Seurat made his first studies to the completion of the painting. Examine the brushstrokes. Note the contrast between the thick strokes of the water, the criss-cross ones in grassy areas, and the smoother treatment of flesh. What words most effectively describe the various types of brushstrokes you can see in this picture?

Comparing Summer and Spring Moods

Does the way the cherry trees sprout and branch, or the actions of any figures suggest movement in the print? It divides into three distinct sections, indicating the use of three separate sets of printing blocks. The shapes of hills, blossoms, trunks and branches extend across one section and into the next. How do the rhythms and gestures of the figures, or the patterns on their kimonos, link the three sections? Does your eye flow easily and naturally across the whole scene, or do you feel the print consists of three pictures which you prefer to look at one at a time?

Tori Kiyonaga, Japanese (1752–1815)
Asukayama at Cherry Blossom Time (c.1785)
Woodblock Print (each sheet 37 × 25.5 cm)
Courtesy of the Trustees of the British Museum

Do you think the mood of *Bathers at Asnières* is similar to that in *Asukayama at Cherry Blossom Time*, a woodblock print by Kiyonaga? (see Flora & Fauna page 86 for brief explanation of woodblock printing.) There is a similar feeling of calm and relaxation in both, even though the figures sit and lie down in one and are strolling in the other. Which do you find the most satisfying two-dimensionally? Which is the more spacious? Which is the most decorative and which the most structural?

Two of Seurat's preliminary studies for *Bathers at Asnières* are on display in the National Gallery. They are small 'on the spot' studies. How do the people relate in scale to the objects and figures around them? Are any of the shapes, colours or patterns repeated or echoed in other objects? Is the scene one of complete relaxation or is some movement provided by, for example, a child playing? What lighting effects are evident? Can you see colour in the shadows? Does this contrast or harmonise with the colour you can see in the sunlit areas?

Links Across Time

Seurat's work shows the influence of Piero della Francesca, who died in 1492. He never actually saw an original painting by Piero, but while a student in Paris, he did see 19th century copies in oil paint of two of Piero's famous Arezzo frescoes. The work of the two artists has much in common. Compare Seurat's bathing boy, who turns away from us, his back half out of the water, with the man undressing in Piero's *The Baptism of Christ* (see page 156). Examine the similarities, and the sense of a controlled restraint and atmospheric mood.

In *The Baptism of Christ*, a cool, clear light replaces the heat of the bathers, but is the calm stillness not close to that of Seurat? Movement is frozen in the art of both Piero and Seurat. You have encountered the same kind of stillness already in that Dutch interior by Vermeer. The historical setting for the *Baptism* is the banks of the Jordan, but Piero simultaneously set his scene in the Tiber Valley. It is still recognisable today. Even the straight road leading into Piero's home town of San Sepolcro, through which the Tiber flows, remains. You can see it in the background of the panel, situated between Christ's waist and the tree. The town has significantly changed, though. Not one of the towers you can clearly see in the painting remains standing today. Many were destroyed by earthquakes. The last surviving one, in the central piazza, was blown up by retreating German soldiers in the Second World War.

The Emerging Genre of Landscape

Piero's beautiful landscapes are a backdrop for the main human and religious dramas that provide the main subject matter. Landscape was not yet an accepted genre in its own right during Piero's lifetime. Half a century later, figures are only incidental to the landscape, mood and atmosphere of *The Sunset*.

The Sunset

The artist, Giorgione, died very young in 1510. Only a handful of paintings are fully accepted as being by him today. *The Sunset*, even if not by Giorgione, nevertheless possesses the unique poetic mood and atmosphere associated with him, and known as the **Giorgionesque**. His output might be small, but he exerted his influence on Venetian art for years to come. On the basis of this painting, try to describe the 'Giorgionesque'.

Note the golden glow of the evening sky as the setting sun disappears behind mountains. The distance is suffused in an atmospheric blue. The foreground is bathed in a warm glow. Is Giorgione so interested in light, mood, atmosphere and landscape that it does not matter who the people are, or what they are doing in this landscape? Two travellers – perhaps St Roch and a companion – rest by a pool from which they have probably already drunk. Look carefully into the pool and its shadowy surrounds, and see what is emerging from the water. Are any other creatures to be seen? Saint George on his white horse is in the middle distance, but was added by a picture restorer in 1934. It is uncertain whether a version of him was originally there. Do you think restorers should 'patch up' damaged areas, so the overall mood of a painting remains, or should they leave them blank, even though this might then detract from the work and even deter people from studying it?

What does The Sunset *share in common with* An Autumn Landscape with a view of Het Steen in the Early Morning, *by the Flemish artist Rubens? One is very small, the other is breathtaking in its panoramic scale and the scope of its vision. The titles tell you one shows the end of the day, the other the beginning. Does Rubens paint the atmospheric blue distance in a similar way to Giorgione? How does the colour and light of the sky compare in each? Is light equally important to both? Do you think the morning light affects Rubens' foreground in the way evening light affects that of* The Sunset? *Compare the moods of the paintings, and consider whether the similarities mean that Rubens knew, admired and was influenced by Venetian painting and the 'Giorgionesque'. Compare the skies and distances in both with those in* The Fighting 'Temeraire'. *Which do you prefer and why?*

Giorgio Barbarelli, called Giorgione, Italian (Active 1506, died 1510)
Il Tramonto (The Sunset) (1506–10)
Oil on Canvas (73.3 × 91.4 cm)

An Autumn Landscape with a View of Het Steen in the Early Morning

Peter Paul Rubens (1577–1640)
An Autumn Landscape with a View of Het Steen in the Early Morning,
Holland (probably 1636)
Oil on Oak (131.2 × 229.2 cm)

In the foreground of the painting, an old tree stump provides cover for a hunter and his dog. Lush trailing plants, laden with fruit, cascade over and around it. What fruits do they bear? Rubens painted them directly and freely. Do you think he observed them directly, relied on his imagination or painted them from memory? A detailed drawing of brambles at Chatsworth House shows just how rigorously he studied details like this, enabling him to paint them freely and with authority.

Allow your eye to travel from these, past trees and over the gently undulating fields, until it reaches the town on the far horizon. What kind of distance does the eye cover on this journey? Is the journey smooth and flowing, or does anything jar and break the flow along the way? Think about the skills an artist must possess to be able to represent such an expanse of space, from foreground activity to the distant horizon, in the way Rubens does.

Based on the position of the sun in the sky, it is obviously still quite early in the morning, although there is already a great deal of activity. Look at how many people are engaged in a wide variety of tasks. One is tending the herd, another is fishing. As the owner of the château, Rubens may have included himself and his wife in the picture. Which two do you think represent him and Helena? Is the hunter likely to be in Rubens' employ? He stealthily eyes his prey, but what is he stalking? Where might a horse-drawn cart be off to at this early hour? Two distinctive birds sweep out of a tree. What type are they? The wide open spaces they encircle might symbolise the same wide open spaces Rubens and Helena enjoy because of their privileged positions.

The building to the left of the autumn landscape in *An Autumn landscape with a view of Het Steen in the Early Morning*, and used it as his summer home is the Château de Steen. Having recently married Helena Fourment, his second wife, Rubens bought this château from 1635. He was so successful, he employed over 200 studio assistants, travelled extensively, became a diplomat, and was knighted by Charles I of England. He is the exact opposite of the popular notion that artists starve in garretts, only receiving recognition after they die. Rubens enjoyed both wealth and status. One of his reasons for buying the Château de Steen was that he particularly loved the landscape of this region and was able to paint it at his leisure.

In addition to the Château de Steen, how much of the land your eye travels over do you think Rubens probably owned? Does it look like rich, fertile land? Try to describe the autumnal mood of this picture. Study the range and variety of flora and fauna in it, and consider whether the mood and atmosphere suggest the land can successfully support and sustain all of these. Does it look equally capable of supporting people, in particular Rubens, his wife, and all those in their employ? Do the mellow atmosphere, lush vegetation, cultivated land rich in flora and fauna, and the range of human activity, all add up to make you think of this painting as a joyful celebration of the environment, and its vital role in human existence?

A Symbol of Industry, Hardship and the Urban Scene

In contrast to Rubens' painting, Marjan Wouda's *Leigh Pit Pony* symbolises hardship and toil in a harsh environment. This sculpture does not celebrate life: the pony is a beast of burden. Sited in a new market hall, it symbolises the proud history of a mining community that has lost all the pits it once relied upon. Toiling below ground, some pit ponies even went blind. It vividly represents a particular environment, but equally belongs within the Universal Theme of **Flora & Fauna**.

What impression does the Leigh Pit Pony *give? What can you say about its character? A noble creature in its own right, do you think it might equally stand as a metaphor for every miner who has daily risked body, life and limb by toiling deep below the ground in adverse conditions?*

Marjan Wouda (b.1960)
Leigh Pit Pony, Leigh, England (1989–91)
Cast resin and coal dust (lifesize)

Introduction

Of all the Universal Themes, **Flora & Fauna** is probably the one you most frequently come across in art in daily life. Look for examples of plants and animals in your locality on places of worship, or on domestic or civic buildings. Find out if any feature on pub or corporate business signs, or on the coats of arms of the city, town, or region. Study the patterns and designs on curtains, cushions, wallpapers, carpets and rugs, cups and saucers, dishes and plates to find examples in your home. Even furniture legs are sometimes influenced by those of animals, either in their overall shape, or by a detail like the turn of a foot. Yours is a most unusual home indeed if flora and fauna are absent from all of these!

Ecological issues are constantly in the news today. Dramatic changes in weather and climate are occurring, and forecasters issue dire warnings about the effects of global warming and rising sea levels. The destruction of rainforests and other natural habitats is endangering plant and animal species that have existed for millennia. As a direct consequence of human behaviour, whole species of flora and fauna are now becoming extinct at an alarming rate. The nightmare scenarios harmful to all forms of life depicted in some sci-fi novels and films, are increasingly seen as real possibilities. All life forms exist in their own right, but the delicate infrastructure that binds all living and growing things together is under threat now as never before. The human race has always been a vital link in this chain and, whatever technological advances take place, this link will remain vital.

Observing and Recording Living Things

Orpheus

According to myth, Orpheus failed to save his lover Eurydice from the underworld after her death from a snake-bite. Grief stricken, he played such beautiful music that vast audiences of birds, animals, plants and trees gathered around him (page 73). In *Orpheus*, Savery uses this story to paint an idyllic landscape in which many species of plants and animals appear to exist together in harmony. The peaceful setting, with no disturbing overtones, is full of lush vegetation, clear cascading water, warmth and light, shelter and shade. Do you feel *Orpheus* is presenting an idealised image of how nature might have been before the tainting effects of pollution and waste? Even a tall distant ruin seems to blend in perfectly, for the flora growing all over it indicates it is already being reclaimed by nature.

Savery shows Orpheus playing a violin rather than a lyre, the instrument he plays in the myth, to a vast audience of animals and birds. Many species are gathered around listening, spellbound by his magical playing, and even the trees bend over him to provide protective shade. Some species gathered there may be too small for the naked eye to see. Might his music equally appeal to smaller insects and beetles? Look at which species of animals and birds have moved closest to Orpheus in his shady spot. Are any closer to each other than you would normally expect, because some are predators and others their natural prey? Does Savery show any creatures normally associated with different habitats or regions? What else appears to be attracting the birds and water fowl to the foreground stretch of water to the right of Orpheus?

The shady foreground area and the clear distance, bathed in a cool bluish light, through which the river flows, divide the composition into strongly contrasted areas. What time of day does the atmospheric light of the distance suggest it is? This paler area forms the distinctive shape of an inverted triangle, with two of its sides leading to the top corners of the painting. The foreground is likewise in the form of two dark, overlapping triangular shapes. Do you find these geometrically insistent shapes in such a naturalistic painting satisfying? Numerous birds are flying in formation, some of them appearing like white specks against the far grey sky. Do you feel these further echo the main geometric shapes? Try to describe the marked difference in how the animals in shade are shown, compared with those seen in full light.

Consider whether *Orpheus* is an imaginative work of pure fantasy, or whether Savery possessed a considerable knowledge of flora and fauna. While working for the Emperor Rudolf II, Savery was able to make many detailed studies of the huge variety of flora and fauna Rudolf brought together in the magnificent zoo he created in Prague. In the process, Savery acquired an almost encyclopaedic knowledge of botany and animal and bird species. The subject of Orpheus allowed him to show off this knowledge to the full and he painted it over and over again. Imagine you possessed a similar knowledge and wanted to show it off, and try to think of other subjects that provide similar scope and opportunities.

Roelandt Savery, Flemish (1576–1639)
Orpheus (1628)
Oil on Oak (53 × 81.5 cm)

Develop the habit of studying and recording animals from life in your sketchbook in the way that Savery does. Orpheus includes exotic species you do not normally see in this country outside safari parks, zoos and, to a much lesser extent now, the circus. Even if you do not live near a zoo, you can probably visit one periodically. Use it as a place in which to study more unusual species. Some might seem docile or slow-moving, so you can draw them without worrying too much about their movements, but others will be far more active, and constantly changing position.

Cultivate the habit of keeping three or four drawings on the go at the same time. Arrange these over a single or double sketchbook sheet so you can move directly from one drawing to another each time the animal significantly changes its position.

In order to do this successfully, spend some time simply observing the animal before you start to draw, and see if there is any kind of pattern to its movements. Are there certain key positions to which it regularly returns? If you can identify any, concentrate on these initially, changing from one to another in keeping with the animal's movements.

Try to combine rapid execution with careful observation, with the aim of capturing both the essence of these key positions and the character of the animal. Do not worry about your drawings looking 'sketchy'. A rapidly executed study that successfully captures a momentary position is of far more value than a finished, detailed one that lacks observation and the feeling of life. Try to spend enough time at the zoo to enable you to study a variety of species. Choose a contrasting variety of sizes, shapes and temperaments. Record them in the positions and attitudes you feel most typify them by being representative and expressive of their nature, habits and movements.

River Landscape with Horseman and Peasants

Aelbert Cuyp, Dutch (1620–1691)
River Landscape with Horseman and Peasants
(probably 1650–60)
Oil on Canvas (123 × 241 cm)

Cuyp was an accomplished cattle painter. Cattle probably feature more prominently in his landscapes than those of any other artist. The gentle, docile nature of cows is vividly captured by the contented character of the foreground herd. Do you imagine the owner, inspecting them on horseback, is probably pleased with their condition? Cuyp successfully captured their character whether they were standing up or lying down. Their reassuringly familiar shapes contribute to the mood of tranquil stillness and calm of this painting.

As well as providing milk, is it possible these cattle will be sold for meat in the near future? What other farm animals and fowl complete this scene of healthy rural life?

Grazing cattle are a familiar sight in the British countryside. Even in urban environments, you often come across the odd open field with a few animals in it. Make studies of cattle, adopting similar approaches to those you used at the zoo.

Compared with some of the more active zoo species, cattle are quite docile. They look contented and leisurely, whether lying down or moving about. Try to apply your new-found anatomical knowledge gained at the natural history museum. While sketching them, try to envisage their underlying form and structure by taking account of anatomical clues. Look at the shape of the ribs when they are in certain positions. When they are sitting or lying down, how strongly does the spinal column influence the rhythmical line of the back? Notice how the shape of the skull determines the form and structure of the head. Do any have horns? How do these relate to their ears, eyes, and other features? These anatomical details will help you achieve greater structure and the essential characteristics of cattle in your drawings.

At first glance, the warm, honeyed mood of *River Landscape with Horseman and Peasants* by Aelbert Cuyp suggests a paradise similar to Savery's in *Orpheus*. Given how flat the Dutch landscape is, do you think the distant mountains could indicate that the scene is imaginary, as opposed to being directly observed? Are there features that appear to be more obviously observed, though? Whereas nothing disturbs the peace in Savery's painting, the calm of this scene will soon be shattered. When you peer into the dark shadows of the left foreground, you become aware of a hunter and his dog. Using the bushes for cover, his gun is already raised, he has taken aim, and is about to shoot. Follow the line of his gun, to work out what it is he has in his sights. This hunter is a reminder that, beneath the surface beauty and calm of nature, human beings are part of the same ecosystem as flora and fauna. Nature is a complex food chain in which each species is dependent on others for its survival, and human beings are no exception. Does this hunter recall the presence of the one in Rubens' *Château de Steen* (see **Environments**, page 69) who is also using foreground bushes for cover. Examine the similarities and differences between the two hunters and their prey.

Predatory Animals

A medieval carving of a griffin with its prey, sited above the main doorway of the Palazzo dei Priori in Perugia, vividly illustrates the behaviour of a predatory carnivorous animal. The griffin is a composite beast that combines the essential features of two different creatures, one a land-based mammal, the other a bird of prey. Look at the shape, form and detail of the griffin, and work out which animal and bird it is composed of. What type of animal has the griffin captured? Even though they are imaginary creatures, do you find the way this griffin is exerting complete dominance over its prey convincing? Does the relationship between victor and vanquished make you suspect this artist probably has observed at first-hand how predatory animals treat their prey and behave towards them once they have caught them?

Carved Griffin, Palazzo dei Priori,
Perugia, Italy (1293–1443) Stone

The Graham Children

In contrast to the griffin, a household pet seems very soft and harmless while it is lying in your lap. However well fed they are, though, domesticated pets still retain their predatory instincts. Just look how this tabby cat is reacting towards the caged bird in this detail from Hogarth's group portrait of *The Graham Children*!

The detail is just one small incident in this painting. The main subject is the four posing Graham children. When you visit the National Gallery, make sure you find the actual painting and study exactly how this detail fits within the whole. While you are studying it, make sure you also have a good look at the container of luscious fruit, some cascading on the floor, that Hogarth introduced in the lower opposite corner.

Describe as vividly as you can exactly what the cat is doing. Take full account of its expression, body language, how it might have got into this position on the back of a chair, and where you think it must have come from to get there. Can you identify what type of bird is in the cage? It is obviously aware of the cat's presence. How is it, in turn, reacting to the cat?

William Hogarth, English (1697–1764)
The Graham Children (1742)
Oil on Canvas (160.5 × 181 cm)

The Wilton Diptych

The constant threat of predators means some animal species must always be alert and on their guard. This makes them look tense and unusually sensitive. Observe how remarkably the unknown artist of *The Wilton Diptych* captures the nervous sensitivity of a white hart. The angle and poise of its delicate head suggest its position is a momentary one. At the slightest sound, its head will dart in another direction as it casts a wary glance. Follow the refined shape of its head, allowing your eye to run round its rhythmical outline. Do not ignore its elaborately shaped antlers. You can easily miss them because they blend in subtly with their background. Study them closely when you visit the National Gallery. Their outline is made by incising into gold leaf and the modelling is stippled on, for they are in gold on gold.

The hart lies on a grassy floral bank, on which you can make out the distinctive needle-like leaves of a well known herb. Do you recognise what herb this is?

The hart is on the reverse of a scene that shows the presentation of King Richard II to the Virgin and Child. Richard used the white hart as a personal device then just as sports teams use emblems such as magpies and canaries today. Could this explain why the hart has a gold crown and chain round its neck? Richard's servants and followers also wore it, as it signified their allegiance to him.

The hart appears on Richard's brooch, and even the angels are wearing badges on which the same hart is clearly visible. What do you think this is intended to tell you about their allegiance to him?

Look carefully at Richard's richly patterned and textured robe. An important feature in its design are the golden harts on the red material. These harts were made by scratching away a top layer of red paint to reveal the gold already put down beneath – a technique known as sgraffito. What other flora and fauna appears on this robe, and in general on the panels of Richard and the Virgin and Child?

The Wilton Diptych
Reverse
Unknown Artist (about 1395–9)
Egg on Oak
(Each wing 53 × 37 cm)

The Wilton Diptych
Richard II presented to the Virgin and Child by his Patron Saint John the Baptist and Saints Edward and Edmund
Unknown artist (about 1395–9)
Egg on Oak
(Each wing 53 × 37 cm)

A Horse Frightened by Lightning

The same kind of nervous sensitivity shown by the hart is apparent in Géricault's *A Horse frightened by Lightning*. Géricault closely identified with horses, and possessed an intimate knowledge and love of them. The tense, still horse, seen sideways on, fills virtually the whole picture area. It is set against the sky, and its sleek chestnut brown coat reflects the light. Instead of being silhouetted, though, it reads as a pale shape against the inky dark tones of the stormy sky. In the distance, close to the horizon, you can see the streak of lightning to which the horse is reacting. Are the white streaks close to its mouth evidence of it foaming with fear? How long do you think it will stay in this position, and what will it do next? Compare it with the *Leigh Pit Pony* (page 70), and look at how they differ physically and temperamentally. You know what work the pit pony has to do. Look at the physique of this horse for clues as to what purpose it is bred and trained for. Géricault was a highly skilled horseman. Do you feel this is reflected in any way, either in the conception of the painting, or in its treatment?

Jean-Louis-André-Théodore Géricault, French (1791–1824)
A Horse frightened by Lightning
(about 1813–14)
Oil on Canvas (48.9 × 60.3 cm)

As with cattle, you come across horses in most environments. Make studies of a horse in your locality that comes closest in temperament to Géricault's frightened horse. Try to capture its character by taking account of its whole manner and stance, as well as facial features like nostrils, eyes and mouth. Draw another horse that contrasts with it.

What sort of work does this one do? How is this reflected in its build, stance, manner and bearing? Are you able to effectively capture the contrasting characters and temperaments of, say, a cart horse, a racehorse, and the kind of pony you frequently see being used to teach young people how to ride?

Equestrian Portraiture

The tradition of equestrian portraiture is a long one. Life-size equestrian statues of famous people are sited in most European city centres. In these, the relationship between horse and rider is obviously important. Horses can make riders seem imposing, thereby emphasising their stature and importance.

Equestrian Portrait of Charles I

Van Dyck's *Equestrian Portrait of Charles I* is the most striking equestrian portrait in the National Gallery. In spite of the small size of head, characteristic of its breed, do you feel the size and nobility of Charles' horse increases your sense of him as a powerful ruler? When you see this work in the original, you will be amazed at its sheer size and scale. If you stand close to it and look ahead, you will find yourself looking straight at the far landscape below the horse's stomach. Even Charles' foot in the stirrup comes above your eye-level. In order to see the king, you must either move back or crane your neck to look upwards, causing him to tower imperiously over you.

Imagine you are commissioned to build a life-size sculpture of a horse, like Leigh Pit Pony, and are making clay maquettes using two of your horse sketches. (A maquette is a small 3-D model of your idea.) Select the two horses that contrast most in build and temperament, and try to bring out these differences in your maquettes. You might be able to make a small maquette just of clay, but you will need a wire armature to support the clay in larger ones. Think of the armature as being a form of skeleton that will give underlying shape and structure to your horse. Do you find it easier to capture the psychological characteristics and form of the horses by building and forming them directly in clay, as opposed to drawing?

Anthony van Dyck, Flemish (1599–1641)
Equestrian Portrait of Charles I
about 1637–8
Oil on Canvas 367 × 292.1 cm)

This obviously makes him seem imposing, but van Dyck also contrasts his bearing and demeanour with the temperament of his horse. Though it is obviously not afraid in the way Géricault's horse is, it is also foaming at the mouth in its excitement, while the king sits calmly astride it with dignity. Do you think van Dyck deliberately contrasts the agitation of the horse, straining at the leash raring to go, with Charles' stillness and obvious skills as a horseman? He died, of course, at the hands of the executioner but, prior to this event, can you imagine those subjects who saw this portrait being impressed by the stature of their ruler?

Sculpture of Alessandro Farnese

If the contrast between horse and rider adds to Charles' stature, a total fusion of horse and rider occurs in Mochi's sculpture of Alessandro Farnese. It is in the Piazza dei Cavalli, the main square of Piacenza in Italy. Dramatic swirling rhythms are a characteristic of this kind of Baroque art. Mochi uses these to unite the flowing mane of the horse with Alessandro's robes, and he then leads your eye back to the horse, where they continue in the magnificent sweep of its tail. As a result, horse and rider become one, with each sharing the characteristics of the other. Do you feel this fusion, in an equestrian portrait full of movement, life and energy, adds to the feeling that Alessandro is an imposing leader and powerful man of action? The monumental base on which the galloping horse and rider stands, ensures Alessandro towers over the people he rules in Piacenza in the same way that Charles looks down on you when you gaze up at him in the National Gallery. Which do you feel is most expressive of power and authority: this fusion in which horse and rider become one, or van Dyck's clear distinction between man and beast?

Jockeys on horseback played an influential role in the early history of photography. The camera revealed the true nature of horses' movements, recording the exact positions of their legs in the various stages of galloping. Today, images of horses are commonplace in newspapers and magazines, and on film and television. Collect a variety of photographic examples, and also video a race, steeplechase, show jumping event, or any other activity involving horses and riders. Select key moments in the event that show the horse stationery, trotting, running, jumping and galloping. Play the video back and freeze it from time to time to enable you to make rapid sketches of the horse and rider at various stages in the action. In making your selection, also try to choose any moments in which you sense a similar kind of fusion between horse and rider to that which characterises Mochi's sculpture.

Francesco Mochi, Italian (1580–1654)
Equestrian statue of Alessandro Farnese,
Piacenza, Italy (1625)
Bronze

Fowling in the Marshes

The close relationship between people and flora and fauna is vividly illustrated throughout art history, extending right back to the cave paintings. The Egyptian wall painting, *Fowling in the Marshes*, was painted in the tomb of Nebamon, around 1500 years before the Assyrian carving of the dying lioness was made. It is another hunting scene, but as its title tells you, waterfowl are now being hunted. The hunter, Nebamon himself, stands in a papyrus boat. In one hand, he is holding up three herons as decoys. What is a decoy, and what is it used for? What similar creature is the weapon in his other hand clearly shaped to resemble? Birds are fluttering about and alighting on plants, and one even perches on the boat. Are these birds imaginary ones, or well-observed, identifiable varieties? Compare them with the deliberately stylised bird forms you can also see in the hieroglyphic writing on the right of this scene.

There is a long tradition in Egypt of using the plants growing in the marshy water for papermaking. What is this plant? A lotus plant, with distinctive waterlily-like blooms, is also flowering in the water, below the hunter's right foot. In addition to the human hunter, a striped animal is leaping upwards as it attempts to catch birds. It is a popular pet today. What is it, and do you know why it was highly regarded in Egyptian civilisation? The painting is a detached fragment of a larger whole.

How closely do the fish in Fowling in the Marshes *conform to your notion of what fish look like? Study live fish in an aquarium or fish tank. Observe their shapes and their markings and patterns. Pay particular attention to the textural qualities of fins, tail and scales. Either sketch them in colour, or add precise colour notes to your drawings. Design a work in a rectangular format on the theme 'Fish'. Show them sideways-on, maybe all swimming in the same direction, but include different varieties of contrasting shapes and size. Either develop your design in clay by building in relief on a clay sheet, or by making free-standing forms, or in textiles using combinations of dying, embroidery, weave and collage processes, or by producing repeat screenprint designs to be printed onto fabric lengths or in a one-off form.*

Fowling in the Marshes, Thebes, Egypt (18th Dynasty about 1400 BC) Painting on plaster (H 81 cm) Courtesy of the Trustees of the British Museum

Some parts were lost in removing it from the tomb wall with the consequence that none of the fish are now complete. Look at the substantial parts that remain, taking account of their overall form and shape, and the texture of tails, fins and scales and consider whether the artist was capable of accurately recording actual types of fish.

It may seem surprising that artists could represent flora and fauna so accurately and in so much detail many thousands of years ago. People lived in much closer contact with nature than is usually the case today. Do you think this probably meant people other than artists were more sensitive to the details of nature than is the case today? The Egyptians record the essence of what they draw, so they always show fish sideways-on. When you see fish swimming in a river, they look very different to their sideways appearance in a fish tank or aquarium. When you think 'fish', is it a top or side view of one that comes into your mind? Which view most vividly encapsulates, for you, what the essence of a fish is?

Long Grass with Butterflies

In the midst of all the richness of flora and fauna in *Fowling in the Marshes*, a number of exquisite butterflies are flying around. There are also fluttering butterflies in *Long Grass with Butterflies* by van Gogh. However, van Gogh looks down onto his subject matter, in the process focusing your attention on an ordinary patch of wasteland. It is the kind of place you probably walk past every day, without even noticing it. If you have a good look, you will almost certainly find similar patches of ground, covered in clumps of vegetation, near where you live! Have you ever looked carefully at these patches, and at what lives in and on them?

In addition to the long grasses of the title, try to find other plant species growing on the patch of ground selected by van Gogh. Does it look as if it is a fertile piece of ground, or do some plants seem to be struggling as they attempt to establish a hold? Is there any indication as to whether it is a still or windy day? The month in which van Gogh painted this picture is known: try to work out which month it is. Do you regard this painting as a landscape or not? Think about which essential landscape elements are present, and which are missing. Perhaps the emphasis on flora and fauna would be reduced if a horizon line and sky were included to increase the sense of distance.

Though van Gogh did not meticulously paint the details of nature, as the Egyptian artist did, he is very precise in the way he uses a brushstoke to represent each stem and blade of grass. What are your initial reactions to his approach to painting grasses, flowers and butterflies? Consider whether you find the painting crude and lacking in detail, or vividly colourful and vibrant in a powerfully expressive way. Do you feel van Gogh is able to convey feelings of growth and life successfully through his expressive brushwork and use of paint? Think about which words most vividly describe the types of brushstrokes he uses to suggest the character of the long grasses.

Select a patch of ground near where you live on which grasses, weeds and plants are growing. Focus on a rectangular area, one or two metres wide, that looks healthy, alive and particularly rich in flora and fauna. You might find it helpful to mark out the rectangle with string, with its edges corresponding to those of your paper. Make a painting of this area, looking down on it at an overhead angle, or even from directly above. You might prefer to combine work done in situ with indoor work that allows you to be more reflective. If you wish to do this, make adequate drawn or painted studies, possibly supplemented by photographs, of the actual site to ensure you continue to work with the necessary knowledge and conviction away from it.

Make sure you spend sufficient time studying the patch to enable you to become fully aware of the range and variety of insects and small creatures that inhabit it. Use them for reference purposes, but incorporate some directly into your work when and as you see them.

Try to invest your work with the same feelings for life and growth you saw in your patch when choosing it, and which you are probably now even more aware of. As well as noting what is in it, examine how all its component parts also relate to each other.

Cuckoo and Azaleas

Like other artists he met in Paris, van Gogh collected Japanese prints. His experiments with unusual viewpoints reflect Japanese influence. In *Cuckoo and Azaleas*, Hokusai focuses your attention on a bird in flight and a bush in blossom. This choice of subject matter reflects a deep Japanese love of nature and flora and fauna. Do you find this print essentially two-dimensional, or suggestive of depth? Whereas van Gogh looked down on his subject from above, Hokusai looked straight at his, as if it is directly in front of him. Is it directly observed, or is it based on memory, or perhaps even imagined? Do you think the cuckoo is about to alight on the azalea, or will it fly past? Observe the detail on the cuckoo. Do you think this contributes to your sense of its flight and movement, as well as showing its appearance? Compare it with the Egyptian water fowl, and think about which you prefer and why.

Look at what else Hokusai included. A rhythmic line is formed where the dark edges of the bush and the pale tone of the clouds meet. The clouds separating the blue sky from the warmer bush colours below it, divide the picture into broad bands of red, white and blue. The design is deceptively simple. Do you find it varied or predictable? Is there sufficient interest in each band? Are you conscious of any formal or emotional relationship between the cuckoo and the azalea? Your eye is led from one to the other, passing through all three bands of colour. Lettering on the print is in vertical lines; is this part of the design, or is it purely for information? You have seen hieroglyphics incorporated into Egyptian art. Think about other art forms that get their message across by combining written information with visual imagery.

Cuckoo and Azaleas *is a woodblock print. Printmaking enables the same image to be repeated a number of times over. It is customary in woodblock printing to cut a separate block for each colour. The blocks are then inked with their colours and printed in sequence, meaning the design builds up colour by colour.*

How many blocks do you think were used for this print? Which colour do you think was printed first, and which last? Does it look as if the printing ink is transparent or opaque? Can you find any evidence of further colours forming by one colour showing through another? Prints have a quite distinct quality that differs to painting. It is quite natural to mix and use each colour when and as you require it while painting. Examine the way in which Hokusai exploited woodblock printing techniques to achieve a variety of colour and texture in the blossoms. Think about how the mood of Cuckoo and Azaleas *is affected by its qualities as a print.*

Hokusai Katshuskika, Japanese (1760–1849)
Cuckoo and Azaleas (1834)
Woodblock Print (25.4 × 18.3 cm)
Courtesy of the Trustees of the British Museum

Sunflowers

Compare *Cuckoo and Azaleas* with van Gogh's *Sunflowers*. Do you sense any similarity between the flat areas of cloud and sky in the one, and the pale yellow background and the ochre table the flowers stand on in the other? Van Gogh was interested in the symbolic significance he felt colours possessed. A single colour – yellow – completely permeates *Sunflowers*, making it a form of symphony in yellow. Is there much variety in the range of yellows used? Black touches are added, but do you think black or brown are used to mix other colours?

Make a painting of a vase of flowers. Select blooms of one type that are similar in colour, but have sufficient variety to make them interesting. Though mainly red they might include pink and mauve flowers, for example, but not blue or yellow ones. Your choice might be based on your favourite flower or colour, what is in season, or the variety that typifies your region, in the same way sunflowers typify Provence and other Mediterranean places. For example, yellow gorse or purple lilac might grow freely near you, or you might have a personal preference for round-headed blooms like chrysanthemums and dahlias, or spiky ones, like foxglove, delphinium and gladioli.

Place the flowers in a vase or pot and locate them in a harmonious setting. If you cannot find an appropriate setting, create one of your own, by standing the flower pot on coloured paper or by using fabrics they naturally blend with for the background. Using a neutral or bluish colour, draw out the composition directly in paint. Fill the whole picture area with the pot and flowers, in the way van Gogh does. In order to achieve this think about how close to the picture edges the base of the pot and the tallest and most widely spreading flowers need to be. Treat the background broadly and simply, but do not let it detract from the flowers. Take account of the negative shapes and the shape of the background where it shows between the flowers.

Vincent van Gogh, Dutch (1853–1890)
Sunflowers (1888)
Oil on Canvas
(92.1 × 73 cm)

Try to describe the palest and darkest toned yellows. Estimate how much canvas area is occupied by colours you would describe as yellow. Other colours are used, but which contrast most strongly with yellow? The whole mood of this painting is obviously determined by its yellows. How would you describe this mood? Think of the range of feelings you associate with yellow, and imagine what yellow signified to van Gogh.

Is your first impression of *Sunflowers* that it was painted slowly over a considerable time, or produced rapidly? The way it is painted is apparent in the brushwork, which is used both to describe the sunflowers, and to express their essential character. This use of paint is equally suggestive of growth. The circular centres are painted in thickly stippled yellow ochre paint which van Gogh used to show the formation of the seeds. Their richly stippled forms contrast with the rigid criss-cross way the background is painted. *Sunflowers* is one of a series of paintings, and van Gogh's bold signature, 'Vincent', on the pot probably shows that he was pleased with this version.

Different stages in the lifecycle of the sunflower are shown in this painting. Some sprightly flowers are not yet fully open, and it easy to imagine them still growing. Others are heavy and ripe, and are clearly in full bloom and at the peak of maturity. A couple hang their heads as if they have passed their peak and have begun to die. Van Gogh obviously had to work rapidly for, once picked, sunflowers last only a short time. He told his brother Theo, 'I'm working on them every morning, starting at daybreak, for they fade quickly and I've got to do the whole thing right off.' Do you think working intensely at this pace, conscious of how little time is available, might make van Gogh more conscious of their lifecycle than if he had just walked past a field of sunflowers with their heads all turned towards the sun?

Floral arrangements as subject matter

Treat your painting as a kind of symphony in colour, in which certain colours recur and echo each other. Note any subtle changes of tone, and variations in how warm or cool a colour is. Experiment restricting the colours on your palette.

If purples predominate, for example, it might prove helpful to rely on a range of blues and reds and to completely eliminate the third primary, yellow. On the other hand, if you feel you are sufficiently disciplined to keep yellow on your palette, use it only sparingly as a mixing colour. Observe how van Gogh introduces unmixed black paint to represent specific floral details. Also, when mixing a colour, try not to use more than three plus white at any one time. This will help you keep the colour fresh, and to relate each new brushstroke to your overall colour scheme.

Constantly remind yourself that flowers are living things. How can you represent them to emphasise they are vitally alive, though already dying? Observe how delicate and varied in shape they are. Try to capture the form and structure of the flowers by dynamically drawing them with the brush, and their colours and textures by the way you mix and use your paint. Work freely and directly, deciding in advance what colour and type of brushstroke is required. Once you have put a brushstroke down, try to leave it alone, avoiding the temptation to smudge and mess the paint about once you have placed it where you intend.

Still Lifes

Still Life with Oranges and Walnuts

Like van Gogh, the Spanish painter Meléndez used a restricted range of warm colours in his *Still Life with Oranges and Walnuts*. The two colour schemes could not be more different, though. In place of van Gogh's brilliant fresh yellows, Meléndez chooses sonorous, rich oranges and the dark tones of earth colours van Gogh consciously avoids using, except in the black on the flower heads – even though these colours are characteristic of his early work. Does Meléndez use any cool colours, or is his still life composed entirely of warm colours? The objects stand out clearly against an extremely dark background, but the vibrant colour of the oranges influences the whole colour scheme. Do you think the mood of this still life would significantly alter if the background was changed to a paler tone or was in a cooler colour?

Even though Meléndez clearly wanted the painting to look naturalistic, he may have deliberately emphasised the geometrical circular forms of the oranges. Do you sense any relationship between these and other rounded shapes he introduces into the composition? Does it include any other kinds of geometrical shapes?

Do you think Meléndez is successful in capturing the texture and 'feel' of orange peel, walnut shells and melon skin? Look at how he treated surfaces like the wooden barrel, the boxes and terracotta jugs. In addition to the oranges and walnuts mentioned in the title, is there any evidence of other natural produce?

Luis Egidio Meléndez, Spanish (1716–1780)
Still Life with Oranges and Walnuts (1772)
Oil on Canvas (61 × 81.3 cm)

The boxes and jugs may be for oils, juices or fruits. What kinds of produce grown in a Mediterranean climate like Spain's are they most likely to contain?

Unpainted patches of cream canvas still show in parts of the drapery. Is a painting 'unfinished', to your mind, if patches like this are left? In contrast to the other still lifes you have studied, the varying amount of finish in this painting provides insight into Cézanne's working methods. In places, you can still see blue drawing-out lines. Can you think of any good reasons why he prefers blue to, say, orange and red? Compare this blue with the one van Gogh uses round the sunflower pot and the horizontal line running across the canvas. Cézanne allows similar drawing lines to show elsewhere. There are variations of line used to describe the shape and form of the melon from which the two gondola-shaped slices on the plate appear to have been cut. Note how he stresses the spherical forms of the apples. Do the fruits relate to each other rhythmically, and to the plate and drapery they are on, as well as to the jar with its raised handle behind them?

A Still Life in Terracotta

Are you aware of fruits and vegetables also being used in the environment? A 'cornucopia' is a horn filled with flowers, fruit and grain. It represents abundance and plenty. Cornucopia and swags of flowers, fruit and grain are often used on buildings. Interesting terracotta examples decorate the walls of the Hyde Park Apartments in London. How do you think this form of relief still life is made? Is it a one-off piece, or does the process involved make it possible for more than one version to be made?

Make an arrangement of flowers, fruits and grain in clay. Build it in half-relief, out of a single large sheet of rolled out clay, or by extending the design across a number of smaller tile-size shapes to be joined together after firing. Try to create a design in which various varieties of flora rhythmically inter-relate and connect, like those in the terracotta version. To invest your work with added life and vitality, use actual fruits, vegetables and grains for reference purposes. It is entirely up to you, though, as to whether you compose an actual arrangement out of these, or use individual specimens when and as you require specific information about their shape or form. You may wish to work out your design in detail on paper first. On the other hand, you might prefer your design to develop organically by working in clay from the start, allowing yourself to respond directly to its tactile qualities.

Floral Decoration, Hyde Park Mansions, London, England
Terracotta

Think about whether the designer began by working directly in clay or by drawing on paper. Consider whether the study of actual flowers, fruits and grain is involved, or whether the end-product is a work of the imagination. Grains feature, but can you also recognise which varieties of fruit and flowers are used in the design? An important aspect of the still life paintings you have been studying is the way each artist captures and records the actual fruit colours. A still life in monochromatic terracotta red is obviously quite different. Look at how the absence of representational colour helps you to focus more fully on the basic forms, patterns and shapes of the flora that feature in the design.

Fruit and Flowers in a Terracotta Vase

Each of the previous groups is fairly simple in that it is composed of a few related objects. In contrast, *Fruit and Flowers in a Terracotta Vase* by van Os is an extremely complex arrangement, full of variety and detail. This even extends to the setting. Van Os did not adopt the common practice of placing the group against a curtain or wall in an interior. A luscious-looking pineapple, placed at the pinnacle of the still-life group, plays a very important role in the overall design of the composition. The whole sweep of the design leads your eye to it. Assuming van Os is working from an actual still life, think about how he managed to balance a pineapple in such a precarious position. Perhaps he just painted one for reference purposes without actually positioning it in the group.

In a work containing such a range and variety of objects, painted in so much detail, you may feel there is almost too much to look at. Allow yourself sufficient time to linger over specific fruits and flowers, leaves and stems, taking care to look at ones that do not necessarily catch the eye immediately, because of their size, position in space, or because they are partly lost in shadow. Which specimens do you consider to be most life-like, and why?

Look at how van Os suggests the bloom on the skins of fruits, and the small globules of moisture glistening on a flower's petals. In spite of all the painstaking detail, does some of this flora nevertheless look slightly artificial? If it does, are you able to put your finger on why you think this is the case? Compare how van Os paints his flowers with van Gogh's very different treatment in Sunflowers (page 87). The contrast between the two could not be greater. Which do you prefer and why?

Jan van Os, Dutch (1744–1808)
Fruit and Flowers in a Terracotta Vase
(1777–8)
Oil on Mahogany (89.1 × 71 cm)

Tulips, carnations, roses, grapes, plums and peaches are included in the wide variety of flora van Os introduces. Do you associate any of the fruits and flowers you can see in this painting with different seasons? Are there some that flower or fruit early in the year around springtime, and others you associate more with summer, autumn or even winter? Beneath his signature, van Os dates the picture 1777 and 1778. Do you think a two-year timespan was needed because of the painstaking amount of detail involved, or because van Os had to wait for certain flowers or fruits to come into season?

In art galleries, you often see people looking at paintings from a couple of metres or so, and then moving still further back to take in the general effect. Van Os makes you do the opposite. You feel compelled to move close to the picture surface to see just how precisely all its various details are painted. When you do this, you rapidly discover it also contains an amazing abundance of minute fauna. You were probably already aware of the bird's nest with its cluster of speckled eggs. But had you spotted the mouse nibbling away at half a walnut, the two butterflies settled on flower stems, or the dragonfly hovering next to the artist's signature? The distinctive black shapes of two silhouetted flies also clearly stand out against the pale flesh of the fruits behind them, while the striped shell of a snail provides a contrast to the multitude of patterns and textures on the skins, petals, leaves and stems of all the flora.

Still Life with the Drinking-Horn of the Saint Sebastian Archers' Guild, Lobster and Glasses

A brilliant scarlet lobster completely dominates the composition and colour scheme of *Still Life* by Kalf. The painting is rich in contrasting textures but, in comparison with van Os' painting, just a few objects are quite simply arranged. Do you feel Kalf records the texture of the lobster shell convincingly enough for you to imagine it will make that characteristic brittle cracking sound lobsters make when they are broken open? Though Kalf makes you aware of all its details, his thick, juicy use of paint contrasts with the way van Os describes objects. Try to describe the character and texture of this extraordinary shell. Concentrate your attention for a moment on the area close to and around its small, jet black eye. Do you find this section of the painting extraordinarily beautiful or amazingly weird? It is quite distinct from anything else so far encountered within the field of flora and fauna.

The painting was probably commissioned by the Amsterdam Guild of Archers and, in full, its title is unusually long: *Still Life with the Drinking-Horn of the Saint Sebastian Archers' Guild, Lobster and Glasses*. The buffalo horn, cleaned and polished, then embellished and decorated, is made into an aesthetic object in its own right. It has a silver statue of the martyrdom of St Sebastian on its mount. Can you make out what fate St Sebastian is suffering? (page 160). This drinking horn still exists, and is on display in a Dutch museum.

Willem Kalf, Dutch (1619–1693)
Still Life with the Drinking-Horn of the Saint Sebastian
Archers' Guild, Lobster and Glasses (about 1653)
Oil on Canvas (86.4 × 102.2 cm)

Among the wealth of flora and fauna so far considered, one category – crustacea – has been absent prior to your discovery of the small snail in van Os's painting. It provides a timely reminder of just how wonderful crustacea are to draw and paint!

The characteristic all crustacea share is that they either have a shell or their skeleton outside their bodies. Which varieties of crustacea spring most readily to mind? Some have wonderfully attractive, detailed patterns on their shells, while others make intricately elaborate shapes.

You frequently find crustacea when beachcombing, especially parts of crabs, and sometimes even whole specimens. You will often come across snails with spiralling shell patterns, like the one van Os painted, after rain on a garden path, on grass stems, or in sand dunes close to the sea. All of these are well worth drawing, but if you ever have the opportunity to paint a colourful fresh lobster, make sure you seize the chance!

Compositionally, this still life is quite bold. The curved horn creates a bold diagonal, moving downwards to the right of the lobster. The lobster, in turn, continues this downward sweep, but now in a counter-movement towards the left. Notice how Kalf then uses a lemon to continue this movement, with it finally culminating in the spiralling shape of its partially cut, unfurled peel. This succulent lemon adds an unexpectedly fresh note of colour, and it looks as if its juice will squirt everywhere if you squeeze it. Among the subdued colour, the red of the lobster and the lemon yellow stand out, and 'lift' the whole colour scheme.

The intense yellow and red colours affect everything else around them. They are reflected on the shiny surfaces of the buffalo horn and pewter dish, and gleam on the wine glass. Are the lemon and lobster similarly affected by each other's colour? Kalf also introduces an interesting variety of contrasting shapes into the composition. Among the most noticeable are the spiralling, twisting shape of the lemon peel and the smooth, flowing shape of the buffalo horn. Crowning everything, though, is the amazing sequence of staccato shapes the lobster makes. Allow your eye to follow and fully take in its complex outline form, but also consider how beautiful each part of this crustacean is in its own right. With its complex variety, it illustrates just how inexhaustibly rich and varied the wonderful world of flora and fauna is!

Personal, Communal, Historical

Our lives are stimulated by events. Wars, for example, affect literally millions of lives, as war memorials erected all over the world in memory of the dead testify. Wars can last for years, but some events are over in a split second. However brief or protracted, though, they all exist in time. Important dates – 1066 and all that – mark the major events in the history of a nation or continent, but events of little importance to others can mean a great deal to you. When reflecting on your life, you inevitably recall those that mean most to you – a memorable birthday or outing, an enjoyable holiday, an examination, serious illness, or the death of a friend or relative. It is impossible to think about some events without recalling the feelings and states of mind you associate with them. These events are important markers in your life. The process extends into the future. You can anticipate events, ranging from those that make you feel apprehensive, to those that help make life seem worth living. Artists use a wide variety of formal means that enable them to show how events unfold within their particular timescales.

Split-second Timing

An Experiment on a Bird in the Air Pump

Do you feel that the strong contrasts of light and dark influence the sequence in which you follow the action? You cannot look at this painting for long without your gaze being drawn to the two girls, and the man trying to console them. Try to imagine what he is saying to reassure them. Why do you notice them? Is it primarily because of the central position they occupy, their charm and emotional appeal, or because the light makes them stand out clearly? Observe the use Wright makes of the interconnecting arms of this trio to make them into a compact, unified group.

The light effects throughout the painting are caused by a single candle, even though you cannot actually see it. Nevertheless, it is easy to work out where it is. What prevents you from seeing it? Are you conscious of your eye being drawn to this object because of the way it is back-lit and brilliantly illuminated by the candle's flame?

Joseph Wright of Derby, English (1734–1797)
An Experiment on a Bird in the Air Pump (1768)
Oil on Canvas (182.9 × 243.9 cm)

Caravaggio used *chiaroscuro* (see page 17) to intensify the sense of drama in a painting. He focuses on an equally brief but dramatic moment in *The Supper at Emmaus*. It is a moment of sudden recognition. Three men, seated at an inn table, are about to have supper. Two are clearly startled. Just look at the man with his back towards you. His elbows jut out sharply as he starts forward, gripping the arms of his chair. You can almost believe the tear in his sleeve is growing as you watch, so sudden and dramatic is his movement. The arms of the man on the right are flung out so wide that the far one is out of focus and blurred, whereas you feel you can almost stretch out and touch his left hand, it seems so close. His outstretched arms are hardly in keeping with the mood you normally associate with sitting down to a quiet supper! Compare the reaction of the standing innkeeper with those of the two men. Is he reacting in a similar way, or simply waiting to hear whether his customers require anything else? The other seated man seems calmer and more composed than the other two. His head is slightly tilted and his eyes are closed. What do you think has caused him to extend his right hand and arm out in such a way, though?

In a film, the incident would occupy just one moment within a longer timescale. If you could wind this moment back a few frames, as you can a film, you would probably expect to see an uneventful scene, with three men idly chatting together as an innkeeper puts food on the table. Think about what would happen next if you could fast forward it a few moments. How will each person be reacting? A bowl, fully laden with fruit, is in the foreground. Its shadow emphasises just how far it overlaps the table's edge, and the men's reactions might cause vibrations that make it topple over. Will the fruit spread out in all directions as it hits the floor? This possibility gives an added tension to a painting that is already full of drama.

Caravaggio seizes on the exact moment when two disciples realise they are eating with Christ, rather than just a stranger, as they at first thought. They recognise him as he breaks and blesses the bread just as he did at the Last Supper. Even so, do you think their reactions are rather extreme? Imagine how you would react, though, if you thought you were dining with a total stranger, only to discover it is someone you knew well but who had recently died! Think about how you would feel if you found this person calmly sitting next to you as if nothing unusual had happened. The fruit in the basket includes grapes and pomegranates. Grapes are sometimes used to symbolise holy wine, and therefore Christ's blood. Pomegranates can likewise be a reference to the Resurrection. On the other hand, perhaps Caravaggio simply wanted to include a still life detail. Which explanation do you favour, and why? Blemishes on the fruit are clearly visible where it has already begun to rot. Might this have symbolic meaning, or was it just commonplace in an age long before the refrigeration?

Comparing two uses of chiaroscuro

Compare An Experiment on a Bird in the Air Pump *with* The Supper at Emmaus.

- *How does each artist use rhythm, gesture and the play of light and dark to lead your eye from one person to another?*

- *Are there more-or-less similar amounts of dark and more brightly lit areas in each painting?*

- *Is there any similarity in the way both artists use highlights to lead your eye to the central drama being enacted in each painting?*

Colours can look rich in paintings that make use of chiaroscuro. Which of the two colour schemes do you find the richest? Observe how both artists make full use of glowing reds, oranges and browns. Which artist, in your opinion, exploits these effects most fully? Though these warmer colours predominate, both paintings also contain subtle areas of cool colour. Is there any similarity in the way both artists complement passages of rich, warm colour with cooler notes of blues and greens?

Experimenting with light

Think of artificially-lit events you have attended, whether as spectator or participant – floodlit sporting occasions, theatre performances, or bonfire night parties, for example. Select one you found particularly exciting or memorable. Relying on a combination of imagination and memory, make a painting or print of this event. Try to recapture its general mood and atmosphere by taking account of the lighting effects you feel helped to characterise it. Try to recall a specific moment when something exciting or unexpected happened. Home in on a group of performers or spectators. Look at how each one reacts and try to reflect this in their body movements, actions, and facial expressions. Are they wearing anything to particularly associate them with the event? What formal or psychological relationships can you make use of to most effectively link the various members of this group together in a shared experience?

Imagine you are in this group, or able to see them through a long-focus lens. Focus on their heads and the upper parts of their bodies, and show their emotions, from ecstasy to despair, through body language and facial expressions. Are they shouting, gesticulating, waving, clutching their hads, or simply standing gaping? How open or shut are mouths, how tense or relaxed the bodies? Ask friends or relatives to assume similar poses so you can obtain the information you require to bring added conviction to your treatment of this subject.

Use effects of light and shade to help you convey the drama of the event. Consider how artificial lighting – floodlights, spotlights, flames – can alter appearances by highlighting certain areas and casting others into shadow. Experiment with light effects by placing a torch or lamp in a darkened place. Explore the kinds of effects you can achieve by varying the height and position of your light source, or by placing it in front of, behind or alongside objects. Observe which colours increase in intensity, and which are lost or become muted in these conditions.

Multiple Events and Narrative

The Supper at Emmaus is about a moment of sudden realisation. Some events unfold over much longer timescales, with numerous related incidents occurring within them. The cup final, for example is an annual national event, but a crowd disturbance, injury, sending off or brilliant goal can be factors that determine why one game stands out from others. Some of these incidents can assume such importance that they come to be regarded as events in their own right.

Christ on the Cross, and Other Scenes

Niccolò di Liberatore shows five key moments in one event in *Christ on the Cross, and Other Scenes* – perhaps six, because of the presence of St Francis in the central section. As the word 'triptych' indicates, the scenes cover three panels and form one altarpiece. This triptych is still in its original gilt frame. The main scene of Christ on the cross is on a much larger scale than the other scenes, completely filling the central panel. Each side panel shows two scenes of equal size, one above the other. The panels are hinged. When the side ones are turned inwards, they completely cover the central panel, meaning each side panel covers half the area of the central panel. Approximately how much larger does this make the crucifixion scene than the other four scenes? The scenes on the left-hand panel are of incidents occurring before the crucifixion, while those on the right occur afterwards. Each incident shown is of sufficient importance to be considered as a significant event in its own right. Indeed, each event shown has been treated many times by different artists.

It is probably easier to tell a story in five scenes than one. Stories in comics unfold scene by scene, and for centuries artists have used similar methods. Most people could not read in the 15th century, but when they went to church they could both hear religious stories and see them vividly illustrated, scene by scene, round the walls in frescoes and through altarpiece representations like this one. Try 'reading' this altarpiece in the same way as you read a comic book story. Can you work out the sequence in which the story unfolds? The first scene, top left, is of the *Agony in the Garden* (see page 141). The main scene is obviously *Christ on the Cross*, and the final scene shows the *Resurrection*. What is happening in the other two scenes? (St Francis, clasping the cross in the main scene, lived in the 13th century. In order to understand why the artist might include him in the crucifixion scene, see page 142.)

Each scene can obviously be looked at individually. Do you think Niccolò also attempts to formally link the five scenes together so that they form one overall design, though? For instance, the diagonal line formed by the cross Christ is carrying in the lower left scene, mirrors the angle made by Christ's slanting body in the bottom right hand scene. Do you think these complementary diagonals occur by accident or design? Try to find further evidence of formal elements like colour, rhythm, shape and line that lead the eye round the whole triptych, and from one scene into another. Consider whether you think the elaborate gilt frame enhances or detracts from the overall effect of the five scenes.

Niccolò di Liberatore, Italian (active about 1456, died 1502)
Christ on the Cross, and Other Scenes (1487)
Tempera and Oil on Wood
(Central Panel: 92.1 × 57.8 cm Wings: each painted surface 43 × 25 cm)

Working in either 2 or 3-D, produce a work of your own comprising a series of scenes, but which also forms one pleasing overall design. Each scene should be interesting and compositionally satisfying in its own right. Base your ideas on a journey you have experienced, but interpret 'journey' literally or metaphorically. However, treat it as an event that sub-divides into separate segments determined by different times, places and incidents. You might choose to start by selecting what you consider to be the most important point in the journey, using this as the basis for a large central image in your design.

Choose four or five other points on the journey and use these to make an arrangement of smaller-scale images round the central one. You might prefer to arrange these symmetrically on either side, as Niccolò does. Alternatively, you might choose to arrange them above and below it, or on all four sides. Whatever arrangement you choose, carefully consider the symmetry of your design by balancing the images you place on one side with related ones on the other. In addition to the overall design, try to achieve formal unity within each image by considering how rhythms, tones, colours and shapes occurring in one might be repeated or echoed in another. Consider how the work as a whole might be distinctive in colour and mood, while ensuring each component image possesses its own colour scheme and mood.

The Battle of San Romano

The Battle of San Romano by Uccello is one of three panels, all the same size and shape and all of the same battle. They celebrate a Florentine victory over Sienese forces in 1432, though, according to some accounts, the event was really only a minor skirmish. Painted for the Medici Palace in Florence, the panels were hung in one room.

Uccello was one of the first Renaissance artists to experiment with mathematical perspective which helps artists achieve a more convincing illusion of space and depth. His battle takes place in a fairly narrow foreground area, though. He does include a more distant view, but this is rather divorced from the main battle scene. Trees and bushes separate it from the foreground action. Nevertheless, Uccello uses the angles made by soldiers' lances to lead you into the background landscape. Observe how the bridle on the black horse on the left links with that of the youth's horse, leading on to the diagonal line of Niccolò da Tolentino's weapon. This is parallel to, and overlaps, the edge of a pathway in the landscape that leads into the distance.

Using the theme 'Processions' as a basis, design a work which has a strong movement from left to right. Try to lead the viewer's eye across the surface of the picture through the repeated use of rhythms, colours, pattern shapes and the movements of people. Your procession can be a formal or informal one, and your approach as figurative or abstract as you choose. In your treatment of the background, contrast the size and scale of the forms and objects within it with those in the foreground. Use the shapes and forms of architecture, shrubs or trees to formally separate foreground space from background space. However, establish links between the two by using the formal elements of art to give an overall unity to your design.

Displayed together, they must have made a striking and celebratory statement about the power of Florence under its Medici rulers. Their overall impact must have been tremendous and quite overwhelming. This was achieved by using patterns, and the repetition of lances, rearing horses, fighting men, plumes and flags, rather than by the development of the action and narrative content from one scene to the next.

On completion, all three paintings must have looked extraordinarily rich. Real gold leaf was used on the horses' bridles, and silver leaf on the knights' armour. The silver has tarnished, unfortunately, making the armour a more ordinary grey colour now. The battle is being fought amongst pink and white roses in a grove of fruiting lemon and orange trees, an unusual setting which helps emphasise a feeling of richness. Uccello's Florentine contemporaries often depicted Biblical and historical stories in the costumes and settings of their own time, but Uccello chose to set a contemporary event in a fantasy world that belonged to the past.

Niccolò da Tolentino, the Florentine commander, is easily identifiable. Centrally placed, he sits astride a white horse, wearing a magnificent bulbous red and gold hat. Try to describe the shapes this hat makes. A blond youth behind him is shown in profile, but all the other soldiers look anonymous, for their faces are hidden behind visors. Once you know who their commander is, you also know which are Florentine soldiers. Rather strangely, this means only one Sienese soldier is shown fighting against them in this panel. Which one is obviously him? Others could be off-stage, but a number of unusually small figures can be seen in the background. Are any of them running away, and might they be fleeing Sienese soldiers?

Horses rear up on their back legs. Do you sense life and movement in them, or do they seem frozen, rather like rocking horses? It is a bloodless battle, except for one obvious casualty. Look carefully at the man lying face down on the ground. If he could get up, how tall would he be in comparison with his companions? Vasari, a 16th century biographer, accuses Uccello of wasting too much time on the finer points of perspective: 'if only he had spent as much time on human figures and animals . . .' Do you agree with this criticism? In your opinion, did Uccello's desire to show a man foreshortened in perspective make him lose sight of his scale in relation to those around him? Pale broken lances litter the ground, but notice how Uccello makes the darker ones slant inwards in the same way as the dead soldier. Allow your eye to continue moving inwards, along the lines both he and these lances indicate. You are led to Niccolò da Tolentino. Do you think Uccello does this to further emphasise Niccolò's importance as leader of the victorious Florentine army?

Trajan's Column

There are countless ways of visually recording events. Trajan's Column in Rome is nearly 2000 years old. It commemorates the Roman Emperor Trajan's military campaigns and victories over the Dacians, and Trajan was buried under it when he died. Different incidents from his campaigns are carved all the way round, starting at the base and extending all the way to the top. Compared to how five scenes are shown in the triptych, what pictorial device is used here? It allows the many different events in Trajan's campaigns to unfold scene by scene round and up the 124 foot-tall column. Altogether, 2500 people are represented in 650 feet of spiralling sculpted scenes. Imagine what these would look like if they were unravelled to make one long, continuous frieze. The carving is too delicate for you to see from ground level and make out what is happening in the upper scenes. Originally, there were libraries either side of the Column, meaning these details could be studied from windows. What appears to be happening in the scenes you can see on its lower section, though?

Trajan's Column (Detail), Rome, Italy (AD 113), Stone (37 m tall)

The Black Obelisk

Just as Trajan's Column celebrates the triumphs of Trajan, *The Black Obelisk* celebrates those of Shalmaneser III, King of Assyria from 858–824 BC. People from all over the Assyrian Empire are shown bringing him gifts in tribute. Each scene contains rows of trees, animals and people.

The king appears twice, once as a conqueror with a bow and arrow, once holding a cup. Can you work out which figures represent him?

- *The inscription records details of his many campaigns. Compare* The Black Obelisk *with the spiralling scenes in Trajan's Column. Do you think the Obelisk also reads from top to bottom?*

- *Is a separate incident shown in each scene, or is one long procession divided up into five convenient segments?*

- *The obelisk and column share a number of similar characteristics. Do you think, though, that the storytelling device of showing five scenes from one event actually makes* The Black Obelisk *closer to Uccello's Triptych in some respects, than it is to Trajan's Column?*

The Black Obelisk, Nimrud, Iraq (c.825 BC) Stone
Courtesy of the Trustees of the British Museum

The Standard of Ur

In order to command attention and glorify rulers, columns and obelisks are sited in prominent public places. By comparison, *The Standard of Ur* is a wooden box, 49.5 cm long. It provides an ideal surface on which to celebrate a ruler's achievements in a much more intimate way. The scenes depicted on each surface are made of inlaid stones and shells. The ceremonial celebrations taking place are in three bands. The lower two comprise animals and servants bearing gifts for their king. On the top row, you can easily identify the king. Like the officials with him, he is seated.

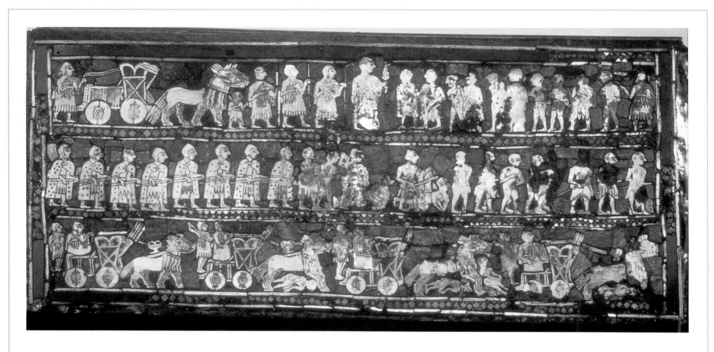

Which figure is the king? How many officials are present? What form of entertainment do you think is being provided by the second person from the right? Study the lower two rows. What types of gifts are being brought to him? The calm of this scene is in marked contrast to the scene on the other side of the box, which shows charging chariots during a battle, and warriors with men they have captured who will be brought before the king.

The Standard of Ur, Mesopotamia (c.2500 BC) Wood inlaid with stones and shells (l. 49.5 cm) Courtesy of the Trustees of the British Museum.

The Burghers of Calais

In contrast to these celebrations of military triumph, Rodin's *Burghers of Calais* is about honour and dignity in defeat. Although it is a sculpture meant to be seen 'in the round' it, too, reads in sequence. The people of Calais have surrendered to the English following a long siege. Six burghers must sacrifice their lives to save their townsfolk from further suffering. In one dignified group, they walk slowly and resolutely to their executions. Though they form a group, each expresses a specific emotion. Rodin leads you in succession from one man to the next. As initially conceived, the men were to stand in line on Calais' town hall steps, though, sequenced one behind the other 'according to their degrees of heroism'.

Auguste Rodin, French (1840–1917)
*The Burghers of Calais (1884–95) in front of
Calais Town Hall*
Bronze (233 × 245 × 203 cm)

Detail

*The elderly man in the centre commands your attention
first. Would Rodin have placed him first on the steps? He
moves steadily forward, head bowed, with a resolve that
must help those around him. What is the burgher next to
him holding firmly in his hands? These have to be handed
to the victors. Is his body stiffened with pride, out of fear
for himself, or because of his concern for what his city
must still endure? Would Rodin have placed him second in
line? It is difficult to do justice to all six men in
photographs, but study each of the other four burghers in
turn as carefully as you can.*

*To what extent do you feel each is afraid for himself, his
city, or is grieving for loved ones he must leave behind?
One clasps his head in his hands, another spreads his arms
out appealingly. What do these gestures tell you about
them? A third raises one hand, but bends his head. What is
his frame of mind? Do you consider all four men are
heroic, whatever position they were intended to occupy on
the steps? Place each of them in sequence behind the first
two according to what you consider to be their degrees of
heroism. Describe as vividly as you can the specific
emotions you feel each of them conveys.*

Crivelli ingeniously combines two quite distinct events in one painting in *The Annunciation with Saint Emidius*. The city of Ascoli Piceno was granted certain rights of self-government, and the news arrived on 25 March 1482, the day of the Feast of the Annunciation. To mark both events, Crivelli includes St Emidius, the patron saint of the city, in the more familiar context of the annunciation scene in which the Angel Gabriel comes to the Virgin to inform her she will give birth to the Son of God. The painting is full of details that relate to both events.

St Emidius, holding a model of Ascoli Piceno, walks along talking to the Angel Gabriel. The inscription at the bottom of the painting, 'Libertas Ecclesiastica', refers to the freedom of the city under the church. Between these words, in the centre, are the Pope's heraldic arms. To the left are those of the Bishop of Ascoli Piceno, and to the right the arms of the city. The Angel Gabriel holds a lily. Think about the symbolism of a white lily in this context. White doves flutter around the dovecote, but the one symbolising the Holy Spirit, borne from heaven on a golden shaft, hovers above the Virgin's head. This shaft, coming from a distant circle of cherubs in the sky, passes through an opening in the wall, continuing its journey inside the house. Compare Crivelli's treatment of space with Uccello's. As your eye is led into the distance, do you feel Uccello's pioneering experiments have born fruit when you see how convincingly, 36 years later, Crivelli is able to create a feeling of depth through his use of perspective?

Some details – the other doves, chatting people – reflect the life of the town. The peacock, perched on the intricately decorated wall, symbolises eternal life. For a long time, people believed peacock flesh did not rot, unlike that of other creatures. Crivelli often included vegetables and fruits in his paintings. Here, a cucumber and apple lie on the floor. Through its association with Jonah, the cucumber (or gourd) symbolises the Resurrection, and is the antidote for the apple – the symbol of Death and a reference to the Fall of Man, because of the apple Eve picked in the Garden of Eden.

The Act of Painting as a Special Event

The Portrait of Giovanni Arnolfini and his Wife

Van Eyck also includes four fruits to the left of *The Portrait of Giovanni Arnolfini and his Wife*. Compare Crivelli's apple with the single fruit, beautifully modelled by light, that sits on the window sill. Though we take it for granted today, it was regarded as a luxury fruit in northern Europe then. What type of fruit do you think it is? (See also page 89.) Van Eyck was one of the first artists to fully exploit the potential of oil paint. In details like this you can see how skilfully he could represent the colours, surfaces and textures of objects, using a technique of painting in thin glazes of slow-drying oil paint on a white chalky ground applied to a wooden panel.

His skill in showing how surface textures are affected by lighting effects makes every object in the painting equally convincing. Allow your eye to roam over the painting for a while, and many objects and details will immediately command your attention. Dwell for a moment on the texture of the dog's fur, and grain of the floor boards, the play of light and shade of the chandelier and far wall, and the crystal prayer beads hanging next to a mirror.

Jan van Eyck, Netherlandish (active 1422, died 1441)
The Portrait of Giovanni Arnolfini and his Wife (1434)
Oil on Oak (81.8 × 59.7 cm)

Using the media and processes you feel are most suited to your particular skills, abilities and ideas, produce an art work as a gift for your closest friend. As a token of your friendship, make your name, in the form of a signature, an essential part of the design.

If you are at your best when creating decorative effects, you can actually build the design round your signature, making it the central feature and integral to the design as a whole. On the other hand, if you feel you have the skill to record the natural world representationally, you might choose to emulate van Eyck and create a feeling of surprise by deliberately using your signature to contradict these effects.

Outdoors: Nature and the Seasons

The Beach at Trouville

We associate certain events with particular seasons. Enjoying relaxing holidays by the sea, and warmth and sunshine mean summer to many people. The sound of the first cuckoo heralds the arrival of spring. Autumn Festivals celebrate bringing in the harvests before the onset of winter. In addition to the demand for indoor entertainment satisfied by places like the Cirque Fernando it also became fashionable to visit the seaside in the 19th century. In *The Beach at Trouville*, Monet painted his wife Camille. It is thought the woman with her is Madame Boudin, wife of the painter Eugène Boudin whose many Trouville beach scenes are known to have influenced Monet. The child's shoe, hanging on the back of a chair, suggests that Jean, Monet's three-year-old son, might be playing nearby in the sand. Look at the clouds and the play of light on Camille's dress, and consider what kind of day it is. Most of this shadow is cast by the umbrella she is holding. The paler colour on the lower part of her face indicates that the sunlight is catching her there, perhaps suggesting she is using the umbrella to keep the sun out of her eyes.

Study Monet's brushwork closely. The paint is freely applied in broad strokes on a coloured ground. When you visit the National Gallery, see how much evidence of this coloured ground is visible in the painting. Has Monet left any of it showing, and what colour is it?

On balance, do you think he probably painted this canvas rapidly in one go, or worked on it for quite a long time while trying to retain a feeling of freshness and spontaneity? A very close examination of the painting's surface reveals a few grains of sand still stuck to the paint. What does this tell you about where and how Monet painted The Beach at Trouville?

Claude-Oscar Monet, French (1840–1926)
The Beach at Trouville (1870)
Oil on Canvas (37.5 × 45.7 cm)

A Winter Scene with Skaters near a Castle

The first snowfall is a winter event many children regard as special. Have you ever woken up in winter to sense a strange, still atmosphere and unusual light? Can you recall drawing back the curtains and being amazed at the magical transformation caused by a heavy fall of snow? Paths, roads and rooftops disappear or become unrecognisable in their new guise. Snow can cause us to see our familiar surroundings anew, almost as if for the first time.

A Winter Scene with Skaters near a Castle by Avercamp shows people enjoying themselves on an icy pond. Young children are playing on it, but the whole town seems to be enjoying being out on the ice. Find the oldest-looking person, and try to estimate their age. The painting is teeming with people and life, yet it vividly captures the sensation of winter stillness and the muffled sound snow creates. Avercamp was a deaf-mute, known as 'the Deaf-Mute of Kampen'. Kampen was his home town where he lived and worked.

Hendrick Avercamp, Dutch (1585–1634)
A Winter Scene with Skaters near a Castle
(about 1608/9)
Oil on Oak (diameter 40.7 cm)

During the appropriate seasons, observe and record how snow, mists and fog or severe frosts sometimes dramatically change the appearance of things. Make a series of studies that document the nature of these changes. Try to record what you are actually seeing, as opposed to what you know to be there. You might find it interesting to choose a familiar and accessible view, *like that from your bedroom window, taking care to first record it as you normally expect to see it. Record how it is then changed by fog, snow and frost effects. Which aspects remain constant, and which change dramatically, or even disappear altogether? Is there any constancy of mood, or is the atmosphere completely transformed by some seasonal changes?*

Try to describe the painting's evocative mood and atmosphere. In responding to this strange, still mood, imagine Avercamp intently observing the scene, attentively noting all the action taking place silently around him.

The scene is so convincing, you could be forgiven for thinking Avercamp painted it outside, from direct observation. It is, in fact, a studio painting. How do you imagine he has gone about it? He may have relied on a photographic memory, or else made use of observed drawn and painted studies of people, buildings and objects, or perhaps he used a combination of the two. Do you think the painting is likely to be a literal record of an actual place, or a composite view composed from various studies of scenes, buildings and objects? Its circular shape gives it a very distinctive appearance. When you look at it, are you conscious of how naturally your eye revolves round it? Do you sense any tension between its outer shape and inner content?

As you look more closely into it, what commands your attention first? It might be the jagged silhouette shape of the tree, and the detail of the birds on the branches, or individual skaters, or small groups or clusters of people on the ice. What details can you make out in the distance? A mist that could turn to fog once night draws in makes everything indistinct towards the horizon. You can sense the vaguely discernible forms of trees and just make out a church spire, but all the distant detail is in virtually the same colour and tone as the sky. The warm greyish sky is mirrored by the icy surface of the pond. The lack of detail in the distance causes the pond and sky to imperceptibly merge into each other. Onto this pale base colour, Avercamp has superimposed the darker shapes of trees, buildings, people and objects like posts and boats. These are all painted in a restricted range of colours. Look at which colours recur most frequently, and which are eliminated altogether or only used sparingly.

Tsukiji

In marked contrast to Avercamp's peaceful scene, a stark mood permeates *Tsukiji* by Unichi. In many places, it is possible to anticipate winter snows with a fair degree of certainty. Earthquakes, however, strike unexpectedly, even in those parts of the world where they are known to occur. An earthquake hit Tokyo in 1923, and *Tsukiji* is from Unichi's woodblock print series, *Tokyo after the Earthquake Fire*, his record of this fateful event. Detail draws you into Avercamp's painting, but this print is broad, simple, and quite devoid of detail. Do you feel Unichi communicates more about the devastating impact of the earthquake through this expressive, gestural approach, than he would achieve by faithfully recording the damage in a more detailed and descriptive way?

Though earthquakes are feared, areas can be equally devastated through human folly. Whole communities are sometimes destroyed as people are thrown out of work as a result of recessions, mergers, political decisions or general change. The damaging scars are evident in many parts of Britain today. Are there mills, factories or mines near where you live that used to be thriving but are now derelict and shut down? Are there empty houses awaiting demolition, or shopping precincts with doors and windows boarded up?

Human acts do not only affect people. You might live near a river polluted by waste and spillages that kill countless fish, and seriously harm whole colonies of ducks, and other wildlife.

Produce a print, painting or collage that captures the devastating impact of an event on a local community, or on the flora and fauna of the area. Adopt a broad, free approach, rather than recording precise details. Try to communicate what you want to say powerfully through gestural mark-making and by composing in bold areas of rhythm, shape and tone. You might choose to use colour expressively and in a heightened way, or express mood and atmosphere by draining it away, relying on monochrome or a restrained range of restricted colours.

Hiratsuka Unichi, Japanese (born 1895)
Tsukiji, Tokyo after the Earthquake Fire series 1923
Woodblock print (15.5 × 11.7 cm),
Courtesy of the Trustees of the British Museum

Like the objects on the top shelf, those on the bottom one are similarly grouped to form a still life. Those on the upper shelf are to do with the heavens, though. A celestial globe complements the earthly one on the bottom shelf, and another instrument is for determining the positions of the stars. A cylindrical sun-dial tells you the date is the 11th April, and a many-sided one informs you it is 9.30 or 10.30. When you add to this information that Holbein's signature is dated '1533', all these clues provide you with as precise a picture of when *The Ambassadors* was painted as you could possibly wish to have!

From first seeing this painting, though, how disturbed have you been by the strange, shadowy foreground object cutting across the mosaic pattern of the floor? It seems far more out of place than the lettering in the van Eyck double portrait, and its effect is really quite disconcerting and jarring. When you next visit the National Gallery, in addition to viewing *The Ambassadors* from the front, also move to the left towards the wall on which it hangs, and carefully look at it from there. From this angle, you will discover that it begins to assume the form and shape of a human skull. In the context of the *vanitas* objects grouped together on the lower shelf, its darker significance and meaning now becomes immediately apparent, for it corresponds exactly with the skull Steenwyck includes in his painting.

Think about why Holbein chose to suspend a skull in space and weirdly distort it in this way. One explanation is that the painting may have been originally designed to hang at the top of a flight of stairs. If this was so, think of yourself approaching it, climbing the stairs. Can you imagine how, in this situation, you become aware of the strange presence of a recognisable skull before you can make out anything else in the painting? Do you think the way it is distorted suggests this is how Holbein envisages you first seeing the skull? When one is standing in front of the painting, of course, it is quite difficult to work out what this strangely bizarre and fantastic object really is. The fantastic and strange are constantly recurring elements in art, though, and the Universal Theme of the **Fantastic and Strange** is the subject of the next chapter.

Myth, Metamorphosis and Dreams

Do you have a lively imagination? Are you a daydreamer? Perhaps you vividly recall dreams and nightmares the next day. Sometimes the atmosphere of a dream seems to be more vivid and real for a time than everyday existence itself. Have you ever become so absorbed in a fantastic story, sci-fi adventure or fantasy film that you have been completely lost to the world for a while, unaware of what is going on around you? Everybody has to escape from the mundane routine of everyday life sometimes, and your imagination is your passport into the wonderful and extraordinary world of the **Fantastic and Strange**. How important is this vast world to you? Its only constraints are the limits of your imagination. It can be poetical and intensely beautiful one minute, or nightmarishly grotesque and full of fearful monsters the next.

One particularly powerful and horrific example is *Two Followers of Cadmus devoured by a Dragon* by Cornelis van Haarlem (page 126). Look closely at what is happening in this painting. One of Cadmus' followers raises a hand in a forlorn attempt to protect himself from a ferocious dragon. It is already ripping and tearing at the flesh of his face. What has happened to his unfortunate colleague, whose body sprawls on top of his? Trickles of blood are running down it, for the dragon's sharp claws are still gripping the flesh, and the poor man's head lies on the ground some distance away. What on earth must the dragon have done to decapitate him in this way, leaving him in this appalling state?

How does van Haarlem capture your attention and draw you into this dramatic event? Is it possible to simply walk past, without noticing this painting? The men's writhing bodies and the snarling beast are shown in graphic close-up. They fill virtually the whole picture area, extending right across it and from top to bottom. In the remaining space, the dragon reappears in a clearing in the distance. What is happening there? Do you think you are seeing another episode from the same story? Perhaps it is the dragon's turn to be slain. In order to make the whole story more clear, do you think the artist included two separate incidents from one story in the same picture? If the dragon is being slain, the background episode obviously follows on from the foreground one. Armed with this information, can you make an informed guess as to what the story of Cadmus, his followers and the dragon is about?

According to myth, Cadmus was the founder of the ancient city of Thebes. King Agenor exiled his son Cadmus until he found his lost sister, Europa. While Cadmus searched, the god Apollo instructed him to follow a heifer and found a city on the first pasture land it lay down on. Everything went according to plan, until Cadmus asked his attendants to fetch water from a spring inside a cave. The cave is home to the god of war's dragon. (The god of war has a planet named after him. Do you know his name?) It is his monster that has killed the two followers of Cadmus. After a terrible fight, Cadmus, in turn, slays the

Tintoretto's Saint George and the Dragon

St George is best known for his triumph over a dragon. He gallops on horseback across the centre of Tintoretto's *Saint George and the Dragon*. The dragon twists its head and snarls back. Where does this enable St George to thrust his lance into it? Any incident involving the slaying of a mythical creature must obviously be fantastic, but the whole mood and atmosphere of this painting is extraordinary. Is it calm, or full of action, drama and movement? Can you see evidence of actual brushstrokes? Is the brushwork mechanical and regular, or full of variety and variation? Look at the pearls in the hair of the woman with her arms outstretched, and consider whether they offer any clues as to her importance and status. Who do you think she is, and why is she there? Is she kneeling down or fleeing from the dragon? Her red dress billows out dramatically, making an almost circular shape. Study it closely, and notice how it is flecked with white, and made up of short, jabby, zig-zag shapes.

Jacopo Tintoretto, Italian (1518–1594)
Saint George and the Dragon
(probably 1560–80)
Oil on Canvas (157.5 × 100.3 cm)

One of the dragon's victims lies dead on the ground. Imagine the body in an upright position, rather than lying down, and think about what it would resemble. Why should Tintoretto use the body as a reminder of the crucifixion? The dragon is close to the sea, and a fort is in the background. A strange light illuminates the whole painting. Try to describe this light effect. Does it affect the whole mood and atmosphere of the work? Billowing clouds encircle a brilliant blast of yellowish light that almost fills the whole sky. What kind of shape does this heavenly light make? Does it fit well within the curved top of the painting? A figure, right hand outstretched, is at the centre of this swirling shape. Who do you think this being is? Is he on the side of the dragon or of St George? St George represents good, so what does the dragon symbolise?

Moreau's St George and the Dragon

Compare Tintoretto's *Saint George and the Dragon* with this version by Moreau. The dragon is right in the foreground now, rearing up as St George, on a white horse, plunges a red lance into it. Think about what the colours might signify. Allow your eye to move backwards and forwards between the nostril and eye of the horse, and the eye and

Find out why St George is always associated with a dragon. The link stems from a 13th century legend. A dragon is terrorising the whole countryside. It is scaly, with wings and a tapering tail, and can only be appeased by being fed sacrificial food. Remains of its victims are strewn around. What is this dragon's preferred diet? A princess is to be its next victim, but St George rescues her in the nick of time. She either looks on praying, or flees as he fights the dragon by the sea. Terrified people often look on from a fortified town or castle. Compare Tintoretto's fort with the castle on top of the rocks in Moreau's version. Which is likely to afford the best protection? Which is most like a fairytale castle?

Gustave Moreau, French (1826–1898)
Saint George and the Dragon
(1889–90)
Oil on Canvas (141 × 96.5 cm)

Compare the dragons on the dish with those on the Chinese arch in Manchester's Chinatown. What similarities do they share? Can you make out horns and whiskers on the heads of those on the arch? Do they possess similar elongated mouths? Are their teeth visible? Their bodies are long and slender, but are there any textural marks that indicate scaliness? How many claws do these have on each foot? Notice the white ball from which lines zig-zag near the mouth of each dragon. This flaming ball, or pearl as it is known, is the symbol of thunder – a further reference to fertilising rain. Look at the dragons on the cloisonné dish again. In the midst of all the decoration, can you see any evidence of flaming balls close to their mouths?

Chinatown Arch, Manchester, England

Dragons regularly appear on pub signs. The Green Dragon pub sign shows a dragon with a fairytale castle behind it. Do you think the dragon has also been turned into a fairytale dragon, no longer to be feared? The smoke from its mouth suggests it breathes fire, and it has a forked tongue, very sharp claws, and a viciously pointed tail. Like its Chinese counterpart, it has horns, whiskers and a mane. Though it is trying to look fearsome, do you find it rather sweet and more like a pet? It has lost its connections with the devil in this more fairytale form. Did this happen to monsters in stories you liked when you were little, or did you like being frightened? Did you like stories about giants, like Jack and the Beanstalk? Which frightened you most, stories about monsters or giants?

*Green Dragon Pub Sign
Lymm, Cheshire, England*

Ulysses deriding Polyphemus

Polyphemus is a one-eyed giant, but at first glance Turner simply appears to have painted a sailing ship against a magnificent sunrise. The title tells you there must be more to this painting than just a ship and sunrise. Look more closely into it, and try to see what else is going on. Is the ship sailing from the landscape, or simply passing by it? If it is sailing away, do you sense any urgency in its departure?

In the atmospheric light, can you make out a vague form in the sky above the landscape, immediately behind the ship? This is Polyphemus. Try to distinguish his shape from the rocks and clouds.

Joseph Mallord William Turner, English (1775–1851)
Ulysses deriding Polyphemus (1829)
Oil on Canvas (132.7 × 203.2 cm)

Paint a landscape, either urban or rural, in which mood, atmosphere, light and the elements predominate. To assist you, make full use of the 'Environments' data already gathered. If you wish, make a vivid sky the main feature of your composition. What effect does this have on the mood, atmosphere and detail visible in the landscape as a whole? Introduce a fantastic and strange element of your choosing. Treat this as incidental, rather than immediately apparent, but try to make it consistent with the general mood of the work. However, you might wish to give the overall atmosphere added significance, once the viewer becomes aware of the fantastic and strange element your work possesses.

Look at what he is holding in his raised hand. In this vaporous light, other details are equally indistinct. Groups of men gathered on the ship's decks are clearly visible, though. What are others doing to secure even better vantage points? Is Ulysses among them? How does Turner ensure he stands out clearly? Fish leap in and out of the water, ahead of the ship, but what are the strange, ghostly creatures near its bow? Look carefully at the area of sky around the sun. Can you make out some barely discernible shapes? These are the winged horses of the sun god, Apollo. To ensure that the sun rises, they are pulling his chariot. The glorious sunrise initially attracts you to this painting, but it is about Ulysses' triumph over Polyphemus. Think about whether the sunrise could have some direct significance to the story.

Polyphemus is a terrifying one-eyed giant. Ulysses is a Greek hero on a ten-year journey following the fall of Troy, and one dangerous adventure follows another. Polyphemus has trapped him in a cave, and devoured two of his men. Two more will be devoured each day. In this desperate situation, Ulysses succeeds in getting the giant drunk and sleepy on magic wine. He blinds him by driving a sharpened stake into his eye, and he and the survivors escape. Safely back on ship, Ulysses taunts the wounded giant, who roars back in pain and anger. In a final gesture of despair, the giant lifts up a huge rock and hurls it at the departing vessel. This is what is in his hand. It misses, and Ulysses escapes. How far away do you calculate the giant must be? How tall must this make him, as gauged by the size of the ship and its crew?

Consider how the sunrise might be relevant to this story. Have you ever suddenly gone into brilliant sunlight out of darkness? The sudden transition can be startling. Remember the impact it had on you. Do you think Turner deliberately uses a glorious sunrise to symbolise Ulysses' escape from a horrible, black end into the brilliant dawn of a new day? It might symbolise the fact that he can now pick up the threads of his life after looking death full in the face. Or do you think Turner simply uses this story as a pretext to make a painting of a dramatic sunrise? Compare this sunrise with that in *The Fighting 'Temeraire'* (page 57). In what ways are they similar and how do they differ? Which do you prefer and why?

Apollo killing the Cyclops

Giants with a single eye in the centre of their forehead were called Cyclops. They retained traces of the sockets where their conventional eyes once were. In *Apollo killing the Cyclops*, by Domenichino, Apollo is killing them in revenge for their part in the death of his son. This, along with seven companion works, looks very distinctive in the National Gallery because of its pale, pastel-like colours and tones. It was painted in fresco, but has been transferred on to canvas. Fresco is a form of wall painting which, in its most permanent form, involves painting on wet plaster. In contrast to the richness of oil paint on canvas, would you expect a process that involves painting on wet plaster to give rise to more delicate tones and colours?

Think about what you are looking at in this painting. Is it a view of an actual landscape or an illusion of one? The artist leaves you in little doubt as to which it is by lifting one corner so that you can see behind it. Erika Langmuir points out that a barred window was directly opposite to the wall it was originally painted on.

Imitating a tapestry enables Domenichino to make this link explicit. The raised corner reveals window bars behind it. A dwarf stands in front of the view, arms folded. He is chained to the bars, apparently for insolence. Do you think the cat is eating his food? Do you find it outrageous that a poor dwarf should be treated like this? Does Domenichino nevertheless portray him sympathetically and with compassion? Do you think the dwarf's lack of stature is used to emphasise how large the Cyclops are?

Domenico Zampieri, called Domenichino, Italian (1581–1641)
Apollo killing the Cyclops (1616–18)
Fresco, transferred to canvas and mounted on board (316.3 × 190.4 cm)

Perseus turning Phineas and his Followers into Stone

Luca Giordano, Italian (1634–1705)
Perseus turning Phineas and his Followers into Stone
(early 1680s)
Oil on Canvas (285 × 366 cm)

Try to work out which of Phineas' warriors are already stone, and which are still in the process of petrification. Do some seem to be as yet unaffected? Examine how Giordano shows which ones are now stone. Compare the colour of Perseus' flesh with theirs and look at how it differs. Do you think the contrasting blue of his clothing makes his flesh look even warmer and more alive? What precaution is he taking to ensure he will not be turned to stone himself? Does Medusa's head look sufficiently grotesque for you to suspend your disbelief and treat the story as plausible? Phineas is on the extreme left behind his warriors. What does this tell you about his character?

Do you think Giordano's use of chiaroscuro emphasises the drama of the story as well as giving the painting impact? Look at the strange jagged edges round the silhouetted figures below and to the left of the head. Do you read these as two-dimensional zig-zag lines? Are the figures still convincingly three-dimensional in their form? Where is the main source of light coming from, and what effect does it have on Medusa's head? Do you find yourself drawn to the head? How does Giordano make use of rhythm, line and gesture to ensure you keep returning to this head? Look at the area of light surrounding it and at how light affects the distant architecture. Is this light natural or, in keeping with the subject, strange and unearthly?

If the Cyclops seemed fearsome, the head of Medusa possessed far more awesome powers. It had staring eyes, fangs for teeth, a tongue hanging out, and writhing serpents for hair. The mere sight of it turned people to stone. Perseus cut off her head, protecting himself from its powers by seeing it only in a mirror. Even after her death, though, Medusa's head retains its power to petrify people. Her head was often painted on shields as protection for warriors in battle. (see page 24)

In *Perseus turning Phineas and his Followers into Stone*, Giordano shows Perseus using this power to secure victory over his enemies. It is his wedding day. He has saved Andromeda, his bride, from a sea monster. She was already promised to Phineas, though, so he and his followers arrive to reclaim her by force. Perseus is outnumbered but, as a last resort, unwraps Medusa's head. In the midst of all the chaos, its awesome powers immediately take effect.

Narcissus

Medusa's power resides in her grotesque ugliness. What causes the downfall of Narcissus? In *Narcissus*, painted by a follower of Leonardo, he contemplates his own reflection. Though you cannot actually see his reflected face, the painting leaves you in no doubt that he is staring at himself in a reflective surface. Its outer rim indicates it is raised up above ground level, but what is he looking into? Is it a glass surface or smooth water? Is it a mirror, a bowl, or even a fountain? Is his gaze casual, or does he seem totally obsessed with his own appearance? Would you go so far as to describe him as transfixed? Why is he so absorbed in himself?

On first seeing this painting, did you think you were looking at a male or female head? Do you think the artist deliberately gave Narcissus qualities from both sexes? Think about why he chose to do this. Do you feel any of Narcissus' features are specifically male or female, or are all of them ambiguous in this respect?

He was, in fact, attractive to both men and women. Do you think his looks are likely to appeal to men and women alike? Is he attractive enough to indicate why he has become so self-absorbed?

Your attention has earlier been drawn to classical profiles (pages 24, 29). Classical values emphasise perfect proportion, order and harmony, and classical portraits are idealised. A person is made to look more beautiful than might actually be the case, and unsightly blemishes are carefully 'ironed out'.

Follower of Leonardo, Italian
(Leonardo da Vinci) (1452–1519)
Narcissus (about 1490–9)
Oil on Wood (23.2 × 26.4 cm)

Narcissus has rejected Echo's love, causing him to pine away until only his voice is left. It repeats the last word of whatever he hears spoken. The wood nymphs, in retaliation, make Narcissus fall in love with his own reflection. He gazes at it in a clear, woodland pool with 'shining silvery waters', until he, too, wastes away. The pool is remote and not visited by either animals or people. The nymphs search in vain for his body, but where his corpse should be, they discover a flower blooming instead. What kind of flower is growing there?

A Grotesque Old Woman

Narcissus is idealised. His beauty and perfection are emphasised, and anything that might detract from it is left out. If you saw a wart on his face, you would probably be shocked. Historians believe that this image derives from a drawing by Leonardo da Vinci, which was probably copied by one of his students. *A Grotesque Old Woman* by Massys, also relates to a Leonardo drawing, now in the Royal Collection at Windsor Castle. The contrast between the two could not be greater. In your wildest dreams, can you imagine yourself considering this woman to be beautiful?

What are your best and worst features? Make two sets of studies of yourself. In one, improve your appearance by idealising your features so they conform as closely as possible with your notions of perfect beauty. In the other, emphasise all your imperfections as ruthlessly as you can. Make yourself grotesque by treating yourself as a cartoonist might caricature you. Everyone is, to some extent, an amalgam of good and rather indifferent qualities. Do you possess any 'Jekyll and Hyde' traits? Perhaps you are inherently kind, but have a short fuse, meaning you lose your temper too easily. Or you might possess abilities which you are too lazy to develop.

Use these studies as the basis for a double self-portrait. Idealise one and endow it with all your virtues. Caricature the other and make it your alter-ego, a vehicle for all your failings. Both aspects can fuse together in one image that has a good and a bad side (see opposite page). Or you might physically separate the two, with one reduced to a shadowy, sinister presence, literally threatening the other. One might be to the fore, with the other hovering behind. One might be frontal, and the other shown in profile or at an angle. Your composition should hold together as a unified design, but each aspect can have its own mood, appropriate to what you wish to say about yourself in it. How much scope can you then allow yourself regarding each figure in terms of expressive colour, brushwork, texture, and mark making? Vigorously exploit all these elements to fully bring out both extremes of your personality.

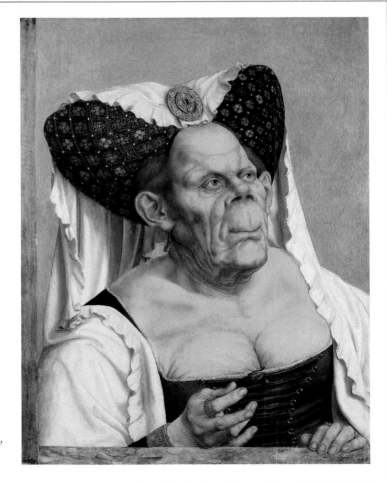

Attributed to Quinten Massys, Flemish (1465–1530)
A Grotesque Old Woman
(about 1525–30)
Oil on Oak (64.1 × 45.4 cm)

Compare her with the idealised beauty of Narcissus. The 'grotesque' is opposite to everything that is graceful and natural. What words other than grotesque fittingly describe this woman's appearance?

Why should Massys choose to paint such an ugly woman? Do you think she is an actual, or an imaginary person? Massys might be trying to caricature a person or group of people, in the way newspaper cartoonists caricature royalty and politicians today. Perhaps the painting has a moral message. If so, what kind of message? Are you inclined to laugh at the woman, or do you feel pity for her? She holds a red rosebud in her right hand. A rosebud is often associated with the first flush of youth. Perhaps Massys included this as a deliberate piece of irony.

Can you sense the shape and structure of the skull beneath the woman's flesh clearly enough to be able to draw it? Would the drawing be an 'average' representation of a human skull, or do you find some of the proportions of her head disturbing? Which are the most disturbing? Those from the eyes to the nostrils, or from her nostrils to the upper lip, or from the lips to the bottom of her chin? Compare these with your own features. Which differs most? What would your reaction be if you met a woman of her age and appearance dressed in the way she is dressed?

Christ Mocked (The Crowning with Thorns)

Try to imagine each figure full length, with the ground they stand on and their surroundings visible. Do you find it easy or difficult to envisage the space each person occupies? Does Bosch's use of graphic close-up make the drama more expressive?

Using this convention of dramatic close-up, make a study of a central person being hassled by a group of bullies. Draw out your design, working out the relationships that link the characters involved. Use idealisation to arouse sympathy for the central victim, and highlight the actions and motivations of the bullies by using the grotesque. Your drawing can be the actual work, or you can use it as a basis to develop your ideas in other media.

Show the central person as the victim, helpless and defenceless. Try to show why this person is being picked on. Is it because he or she stands out from the peer group in some obvious way? Try to capture the isolation, vulnerability and fear the person is feeling. Use gestures, expressions and rhythm to indicate how the bullies are threatening the person's space.

Who are the bullies? What individual personality traits motivate them? Why do they operate together, picking on one person at a time? Think of the effects of their bullying characteristics on the way they look, move and act. Are you going to include a ring leader? Is one a weak side-kick, or hanger-on? Emphasise such traits by using exaggeration and distortion expressively, as Bosch did. Bring out individual characteristics while emphasising their collective weakness. Allow yourself the necessary licence to produce a work with a powerful message forcibly expressed through your use of the fantastic and strange.

Hieronymus Bosch, Netherlandish (living 1474, died 1516)
Christ Mocked (The Crowning with Thorns)
(about 1490–1500)
Oil on Oak (73.5 × 59.1 cm)

Idealisation and the grotesque blend in *Christ Mocked (The Crowning with Thorns)* by Hieronymus Bosch. Five heads completely fill the picture, as if being seen through a camera's zoom lens. All unnecessary detail is eliminated. The neutral colour and absence of detail in the background make it totally incidental to the human drama. Which of the five heads is idealised? Is the mood and atmosphere of the central area occupied by Christ in keeping with, or in contrast to the surrounding areas? Does the work read as a unified design? Do you feel Christ is staring at you, or past you into space? What does he appear to be thinking and feeling? One of his tormentors is about to ram the crown of thorns down onto his head. How is he reacting to the indignity? What does the crown of thorns resemble?

One tormentor occupies each corner of the painting. Two are shown three-quarter view, and two are in profile. They look very unpleasant. Are they all equally grotesque, or do some look worse than others? Is one a ring leader, or are they all equally willing and active participants? Focus on each in turn, and think about what form of mockery each is indulging in? What kind of person is he? Examine his expression and body language for clues about what he is thinking and feeling. What is he doing, or is about to do? Why is he behaving like this? Imagine you are in Christ's unenviable position, with these men taunting you and crawling all over you. Which man poses the biggest threat? Which is most repellent? Which is the most despicable and which arouses your pity? One is wearing a spiked dog collar possibly because Christ's tormentors were likened to savage dogs. Think about the symbolic significance of other objects and motifs on the tormentors.

Abstract Shapes and Visionary Events

The Agony in the Garden Of Gethsemane

El Greco's use of trees, hills and branches in *The Agony in the Garden of Gethsemane* is in complete contrast to the way Bosch virtually eliminated space in *Christ Mocked*. El Greco uses an inky sky and full moon to show it is night. Compare the clouds with the landscape elements, though. Does El Greco convey the texture of each, or do both clouds and rock appear to be made of similar substances? Look at the strange object three disciples, Peter, James and John, lie sleeping in. Is it a smooth, ovoid cave, like a hollowed-out half egg? Imagine the figures purely as colours and shapes for a moment, while allowing your eye to revolve round the painting. Sense the relationship between the clouds and the boulder behind Christ. Look at the dark shapes the sky makes and notice how these link with the right side of the boulder in shadow. Observe the way highlights sharply meet shadows on garments like Christ's robe. Are you conscious of looking at a strangely abstract painting in the shapes, forms and rhythms it makes?

The sleeping disciples form odd, swirling shapes. Are they lying on or against anything for comfort? Could they even lie in that space in those positions? The whole painting is full of strange contradictions and inconsistencies. If the disciples and Christ stood together, side by side, how would their size compare with his?

An angel kneels on top of the cave, above the disciples. Assuming they are of average height, how tall must the angel be? How do the distant soldiers compare in size to Christ or his disciples? Why are they approaching and what threat do they pose? Christ has asked God if he must be sacrificed, adding, 'nevertheless not my will, but thine, be done'. An angel is sent from heaven to give him strength. El Greco shows the angel symbolically holding the cup of grief Christ asks God to take from him. The soldiers arrest Christ. A chain of events is set in motion that culminates in his crucifixion. Bosch's depiction of Christ mocked and crowned with thorns is but one event in this chain.

The Stigmatisation of St Francis

El Greco's *Agony in the Garden* is a visionary, rather than a literal, interpretation of an event. Is St Francis experiencing a vision, or actually seeing an angel, in Sassetta's *The Stigmatisation of St Francis*? Whichever it is, the five wounds Christ received on the cross now also appear on St Francis. Two are clearly visible in the painting. Where are they? What caused these marks on Christ's body in the first place? St Francis receives the stigmata on 14 September 1224 at La Verna, high in the Tuscan mountains above San Sepolcro, (see page 000) the town for which the painting was executed. It is one panel from a very large altarpiece and six others, all showing episodes in the life of St Francis, are also in the National Gallery.

Does St Francis' pose strike you as unusual? He kneels, his hands raised towards the angel, perfectly positioned to receive the stigmata. If you ever visit this area of Italy, you will see many similar versions of St Francis, for Sassetta makes use of a commonly used stigmatisation pose. Is the stigmatisation the only miracle taking place? St Francis was probably praying in front of the wooden cross as the angel appeared. What is happening to this cross now? Examine the reaction of his companion, Brother Leo. St Francis was apparently alone when this event occurred. Why do you think Brother Leo is also shown in most versions of this incident? La Verna still attracts many pilgrims. Are you aware of any recent miracles, and are these also likely to attract people to the sites where they took place?

- *How many wings does the angel appear to have?*
- *How would you describe the shape of the angel and that surrounding it?*
- *What event do the outstretched arms echo?*
- *Are there times of the day or night when you think visions and miracles are more likely to occur?*
- *What time of day does it appear to be in the painting?*
- *Consider whether the main source of light comes from the angel, or whether the setting sun, low in the sky, is equally likely to create the warm glow of light and strong shadows on the distant mountains. Try to find other examples of cast shadows in the painting. Do you feel Sassetta's use of light and shade is consistent throughout the picture?*

Stefano di Giovanni, called Sassetta, Italian (1392?–1450)
The Stigmatisation of Saint Francis
(1437–44)
Tempera on Poplar (87.5 × 52.5 cm)

Reality and Metamorphosis

Apollo and Daphne

The stigmata p hysically changed St Francis, making him like a second Christ to his followers. Look at the physical change that alters Daphne in *Apollo and Daphne* by Pollaiuolo. In changing from one state to another, she becomes a weird mixture of human and floral elements, the sprouting branches resembling wings or parachutes. She seems to be flying, sweeping up Apollo in the process. A landscape with a winding river recedes into an atmospheric distance. It is the Arno Valley region of Tuscany, well known to the artist. Apollo and both the human and floral parts of Daphne are treated in an equally convincing realistic manner. Do you think this naturalistic treatment makes Daphne's transformation into a laurel tree seem even more strange than if it were painted in the kind of abstract, visionary way preferred by El Greco?

Why is this fate befalling Daphne? The god Apollo has mocked Cupid's puny weapons. In revenge, Cupid fired an arrow that made Apollo fall in love with Daphne. Another arrow fired at Daphne, however ensures she will never fall in love. Captivated by her beauty, Apollo cannot accept her rejections and tries to force himself on her.

Produce a work on the theme, 'Metamorphosis'. You have probably noticed how cloud shapes can sometimes resemble people, animals or objects. The same is often true of gnarled and twisted tree trunks and root systems. Make studies of roots, branches and trunks that are distinctive in their character and shape.

Allow your imagination sufficient scope to enable you to sense other forms and objects in them. Substantiate your observations by making textural rubbings from bark and grainy surfaces, and allow your imagination to shape these into objects, too. Use this information to make either a two or three-dimensional work. Emphasise the ambiguities, and make it a study of a natural form that is also a representation of an animal or human shape.

Antonio del Pollaiuolo, Italian (about 1432–1498)
Apollo and Daphne (probably 1470–80)
Oil on Wood (29.5 × 20 cm)

She flees, but he gives chase. As he is about to catch her, she cries out to her father to save her. Thin bark begins to enclose her chest, her hair grows into leaves, her feet begin to take root, and her face becomes a treetop. Her arms also turn into branches, and it is this aspect of the metamorphosis emphasised by Pollaiuolo.

Cupid Complaining to Venus

Cupid appears in Cranach's painting, *Cupid Complaining to Venus*. He is the son of Venus. Do you know who Venus is? An inscription in the top right corner of the picture says: 'While Cupid was stealing honey from the hollow of a tree-trunk, a bee stung the thief in the finger. Even so does brief and transient pleasure which we seek harm us with sadness and pain.' Venus mocks Cupid: the wounds of love he inflicts on others hurt far more than any bee's sting. Some bees are still on Cupid, but what is he holding? A beautiful landscape in the distance is mirror-imaged in the still water. Compare this section with Patenier's landscape in '*Saint Jerome in a Rocky Landscape*' (page 50). Do you feel they have much in common?

Compare Cranach's Venus with Velázquez' Rokeby Venus *(page 31), which also includes Cupid. Which version do you feel is most chaste and which most provocative? Why does she seem so much more strange and fantastic in the Cranach?*

Look at her extraordinarily elaborate headdress and consider her pose? Does it appeal to your ideas of elegance and sophistication? She lifts her left foot and holds the branch of a ripely laden apple tree with a raised hand. Do you think the apple tree might be added to make a link between Venus and Eve?

Cranach emphasises the even paleness of her skin, making it stand out by surrounding her whole body with very dark foliage. Do you think this Venus is a 16th century version of the fashion models and pin-ups reproduced in magazines and newspapers today?

What kind of person do you think would commission a painting of this kind, or employ an artist like Cranach? Think about where and how you would expect a painting like this to be displayed

Lucas Cranach the Elder, German (1472–1553)
Cupid Complaining to Venus
(probably early 1530s)
Oil on Wood (81.3 × 54.6 cm)

An Allegory with Venus and Cupid

It is thought Duke Cosimo de' Medici of Florence sent Bronzino's *An Allegory with Venus and Cupid* as a gift to King Francis I of France. As its title indicates, Venus and Cupid appear yet again in this work. It is the most frankly erotic painting in the National Gallery. Compare this Cupid with the innocent young boy in Cranach's painting. Does this knowing Venus make Cranach's version seem charmingly naive and innocent? The work is a sort of puzzle, full of complex and obscure meanings. Langmuir suggests that in a pleasure-loving court like that of Francis, unravelling its symbolism would be an ideal 'excuse for admiring at length the alluring bodies of Venus and Cupid', and the explicit detail of their embrace.

Venus clasps a golden apple she has won in her left hand. Do you know how she won it? With Cupid's thoughts otherwise engaged, she steals an arrow from his quiver, and is about to pierce one of his wings with it. Which of his special powers will he lose if she succeeds? What is the laughing boy going to throw at them? He has dancing bells around one ankle, but seems unaware of the thorn sticking in his other foot.

Bronzino's work incorporates opposites and dark and light, so what might the two theatre masks at Venus' feet symbolise? What could the mask worn by the figure in the top left corner denote? Time holds out a brilliant blue sheet behind the group, as if to protect everybody. Think about what his hourglass represents.

The most obviously disturbing feature is the man in shade to the left of Cupid. He clutches his head and, from his wide open mouth he utters a cry of despair. Does he represent jealousy or envy? He is widely associated with these emotions, but a recent interpretation links him with sexually transmitted disease. Could he be expressing a 16th century fear of venereal disease similar to the 20th century horror of AIDS?

Agnolo di Cosimo, called Bronzino,
Italian (1503–1572)
An Allegory with Venus and Cupid
(probably 1540–50)
Oil on Wood (146.1 × 116.2 cm)

Behind him lurks a monster with a human face and a reptile's body. It tantalisingly offers up a honeycomb with one hand, but hides a sting in its tail with the other. It represents Pleasure which, on the surface, the painting seems to be about. Life has a darker side, though, and each pleasure symbol seems to be matched by a negative one. The depressing message of the work seems to be that all life's pleasures cause pain and suffering.

A Satyr mourning over a Nymph

An Allegory with Venus and Cupid is meant to puzzle. The meaning in Piero di Cosimo's *A Satyr mourning over a Nymph* is obscure because nobody knows for certain which myth it illustrates. It is one of the most gentle, poetical paintings in the National Gallery. Consider which elements contribute most to its tender mood. It may be the limpid atmosphere of the bluish distance, or perhaps the peaceful vision of nature expressed through delicate flora and the distant birds and animals. Is it the tender compassion shown by the mourning dog, or is it the way the kneeling satyr gently caresses the dead woman lying on the grassy earth? Based on your observations of this particular mourner, try to define a satyr.

Piero di Cosimo, Italian (about 1462–after 1515)
A Satyr mourning over a Nymph (about 1495)
Oil on Poplar (65.4 × 184.2 cm)

Wounds are visible on the nymph's neck and wrists. How did she receive these? She is obviously young. How old does her appearance suggest she is? What was her relationship to the dog and satyr? Do you think they witnessed her death, or have they found her already dead, lying in this position? Think about what the dog and satyr are likely to do next. It has been suggested that the painting is based on a myth warning against jealousy and mistrust.

Based on these questions, and any others you might wish to ask, write a myth that tells the story of 'A Mythological Subject'. Take into account all the clues and details to be found in the painting. Weave these into a fantastic and strange story that is as vivid, plausible and gripping as you can make it.

Mahakala, Protector of Science

Mahakala is an aspect of the Hindu god Shiva. A Tibetan banner painting of him is full of dark turbulence and flickering, agitated shapes. It is a dramatic contrast to the calm of *A Satyr mourning over a Nymph*. Shiva has two aspects, one calm the other wrathful. There is no doubt which Mahakala represents! A prostrate figure lies under his feet as he wages war on demons. Are the two small white figures that jab at him from either side, demons? What are the weapons he wields in either hand? He can shoot flames from the third eye in the centre of his head. Are the flickering red shapes surrounding him fire? He has five skulls on top of his head, but what is he wearing round his waist?

The surroundings consist of a rich variety of textural patterns and shapes. Do you think earth, air, fire and water are all represented in these? Five seated gods and Buddhist notables are looking down on the action. Are they sitting up in the clouds? The two small circular shapes in the sky might represent the sun and moon. Look closely at the amazing flurry of activity going on at the bottom of the picture. Taking account of the variety of fantastic creatures, people and shapes you can make out, how would you describe this scene to capture its mood?

Find the two other images in this chapter you think are the most fantastic and strange. Compare them to this banner.

- *Which of the three is the most fantastic in its treatment?*

- *Which makes the strangest combination of patterns, textures, shapes and forms?*

- *Which do you feel is the most dramatic?*

- *Which conjures up the most fantastic and strange mood and atmosphere?*

- *Think about which is your favourite, and which you like the least, and explain why.*

Mahakala as 'Protector of Science', Tibet (18th century)
Banner painting (86.5 × 56.0 cm)
Courtesy of the Trustees of the British Museum

147

Introduction: Form and Meaning

Dillian Gordon describes Picasso's *Fruit Dish, Bottle and Violin* as the 'first abstract painting to be acquired by the National Gallery'. By definition, this means the rest of the collection is not abstract, or at least not in the same sense as this Cubist work. According to Herbert Read, however, 'All art is primarily abstract'. 'We must not be afraid of this word "abstract",' he wrote. Leonardo da Vinci insisted every part of a work of art must be in proportion to the whole; it is beautiful harmonies that hold us 'spellbound in admiration', producing 'a joy without parallel and superior to all other sensations'. Visual harmonies of this kind satisfy us at a purely sensory, abstract level, whatever else a work of art might or might not also be about.

Peter and Linda Murray suggest that a 'philosophical justification of abstract art may be found in Plato', who maintained that beauty of shape is not found in living creatures, as most people might expect, but in 'straight lines and curves and the surfaces or solid forms produced out of these by lathes and rulers and squares'. Plato considered this geometric beauty to be constant, natural and absolute. If this kind of abstract basis did not exist in art prior to Picasso in the 20th century, 'The Abstract' would not qualify as a Universal Theme. However, an innate human desire for harmony and order is to be found in art from all times, places and cultures, and this makes 'The Abstract' the fitting Universal Theme with which to conclude.

Abstract Design in the Environment

In fine art, abstract works often generate controversy, but purely abstract forms and shapes are often more readily accepted when used in environmental art. Most people are able to respond positively to harmonious arrangements of geometric pattern shapes like those formed by the design of the roof tiles of St Stephen's Cathedral in the centre of Vienna. Our reaction is rather like that described by Plato, unworried by concerns as to what the design might mean or represent. The effect resides in colours and shapes that are pleasing to the eye, with your response determined purely by the visual pleasure derived from looking at it.

Note down all the abstract forms, patterns and shapes you can find in your locality. What, for example, is there between home and school? Record examples in your sketchbook. Where possible, also photograph and include in your sketch or ideas book, abstract details like that of the cathedral door.

To fully familiarise yourself with exactly what is around you when out walking, cultivate the habit of looking up, down, and around you, as well as at what is just directly in front of you. You will probably be surprised at how much there is of genuine interest, and how unaware of this you previously were. You may even find yourself taking a renewed interest in places you previously considered dull and uninteresting.

As well as making you more visually aware – a valuable asset in its own right – you will probably find this form of study also makes you aware of an increased range of possibilities with regard to your own art practice.

St. Stephen's Cathedral Roof, Vienna, Austria

Anglican Cathedral Door, detail, Liverpool, England

Most visitors to Vienna become aware of this roof pattern while still a considerable distance from the cathedral, but a close scrutiny of architectural details often reveals similar abstract qualities that often pass unnoticed. The sheer mass of Liverpool's Anglican Cathedral façade makes it easy to overlook smaller details like its doors. Their geometric, regular repeat pattern shapes are beautifully offset by the organic texture of the wood grain. These rigidly angular panel shapes also contrast with the circular form of the decorative bolts which, in addition to their functional role, play an important part in the overall design of the door. Look at the door lock, which is obviously functional. Do you think its position is determined by purely practical considerations, or do you feel the designer has also considered its abstract relationship to the other geometric forms that surround it?

Asante Silk Textile

The abstract use of patterns and shapes in textile designs is quite commonplace. Find examples on carpets, rugs, curtains, cushions and other furnishings in your own home. Are any of your clothes made from materials with non-figurative designs or patterns on them?

Abstract shapes of a rectangular and zig-zagging nature characterise the Asante silk weavings of Ghana. The fresh, clear red, yellow and green, offset by textural notes of black, used in this example are typical of the bold use of colour you will find in most Asante weaving. The repeat nature of the design is obviously most apparent when the material is evenly spread out. Made to be worn, though, it is easy to imagine how striking the design will look once the material falls into natural rhythms and folds round the human body. This particular example is made to be worn by a senior Asante person on important ceremonial occasions.

Asante Silk Textile, Ghana
Weaving
Courtesy of the Trustees of the British Museum

Design an abstract textile piece, using any process or combination of processes you wish. You can make a simple warp and weft construction, or work in felt, batik, fabric collage, or by using paper stencil shapes as the basis for a screenprint.

Experiment by composing the pattern using combinations of geometric shapes. Arrange these in relation to one another, making them touch, overlap or repeat in various ways, but always taking care to ensure you take account of the negative shapes they leave, as well as the positive ones they make.

If you wish to print red circles and purple triangles on a white ground, for example, pay attention to the white shapes that appear, as much as to the more obvious red and purple ones.

Though geometric forms are basic to the design, you do not necessarily have to complete them. You might, for example, prefer to compose in arcs, rather than whole circles. If you wish, you can make your geometric shapes less insistent and more irregular by drawing them directly and freely, with the aim of giving your design a softer, more organic feel.

Maori War Canoe

As well as forming attractive patterns and shapes, the above examples are abstract in the sense they have no obvious subject matter. The boundaries between abstract and figurative art can be indistinct, though. The design on the prow of a Maori war canoe looks, at first glance, to be made up of purely abstract shapes. However, in reality it consists of several *manaia*, a recurrent image in Maori carving. *Manaia* is a motif that combines elements of man, bird and lizard. Once you are aware of this, you can probably identify features within the detail of its intertwining forms associated with either a man, bird or lizard. Imagine you are at sea, and a war canoe with a prow like this passes by, with the light behind it. It will obviously be silhouetted, but do you think the repeat nature of the negative shapes that show up where the light passes through the gaps, will be impressive, although of an essentially abstract nature? Do you think any distinction between *manaia* and the abstract is likely to exist in the mind of a Maori, on seeing this prow today?

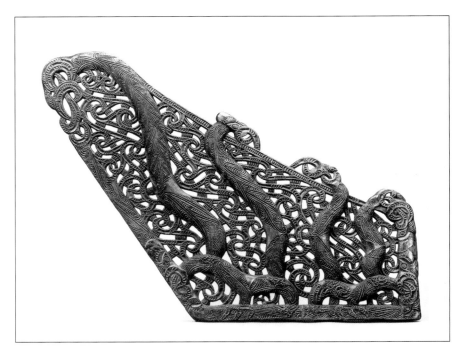

Prow of Maori War Canoe, New Zealand (Probably 18th or 19th century) Wood (89 cm)
Courtesy of the Trustees of the British Museum

Chilkat Dancing Blanket

A similar blurring of boundaries characterises the conception and design of a Native American Chilkat blanket from the northwest coast of North America. It is made from natural materials and fibres, including twined wool and vegetable fibre. Men and women both have clear and quite distinct roles to play in the making of these blankets. Though traditionally woven by women, the design is directly copied from an image painted on a wooden pattern board by a man. The woman works directly from this pattern board, by propping it up alongside her weaving.

Though the design is boldly abstract, it has great meaning and significance to its people. This example is a dancing blanket, made to be worn by a man of high rank at a feast and, like all such Chilkat blankets, it is based on the crest animal of the people. Their crest animal was originally painted on the walls of their houses, and in this context retains the recognisable outline shape of the animal.

In order to fill every bit of the blanket, though, the various parts of the animal are broken up, distorted and arranged all over its surface to create a complete abstract design. In this form, it is usually impossible to identify the animal it represents. Can you work out which feature the pronounced ovoid shapes probably denote, though?

The all-over design is obviously striking when the blanket is spread out as a two-dimensional form. However, the central section is designed to cover the wearer's back. This signifies the front view of the crest animal, while both end sections are sideways representations of it. Native Americans believe in the oneness of all creatures, animal and human, and their myths frequently tell of transformations from one state to another. Completely cloaked in his blanket, wearing a mask, imagine how, to those present, the owner actually becomes the three-dimensional representation of the animal for the duration of the dance. Not only are the abstract shapes and their meaning inseparable, art and life are inextricably linked.

Fruit Dish, Bottle and Violin

Picasso treats still life objects in *Fruit Dish, Bottle and Violin* in a similar way. He breaks them up, distorts them and arranges them all over the picture surface in an equally abstract manner. Dillian Gordon argues that this painting is a 'rejection of the entire Western tradition of the previous six centuries'. It ignores the 'rules of linear and aerial perspective, the modelling of an object with a consistent source of light, and virtuoso painterly technique'. You can see ample evidence of all these in this book. In contrast, Picasso emphasises the two-dimensional surface of the picture, without attempting to create depth or space, except where you know one shape must be behind another because of overlapping. Each object is reduced to a flat, decorative shape of texture, colour or tone. You know no attempt is made to 'match' the prominent green, blue and lilac patches to actual colours in the group. Although the colour is not representational, Picasso's choice of greens, blues and lilacs might indicate their presence in the actual group, however modified they have become.

Though his main interest seems to be in the geometric shapes the objects make, Picasso does give you some clues as to what the objects are. You can recognise the fringe on a rug, a table leg, and lettering on a bit of newspaper. Can you tell what shape the fruit bowl is, or what types of fruit are in it? Though the violin is disjointed, you can work

Set up a still life group of your own. Compose it using everyday kitchen and household objects, like jugs, bottles or bowls. Include fruit, and objects that provide textural contrast, just as Picasso introduced, for example, newsprint and a rug fringe to provide contrast with the other objects used. You might also select an object that is distinctive in its form and shape, to fulfil the kind of function the violin performs in Fruit Dish, Bottle and Violin. *Arrange the group with a view to showing some objects to best advantage sideways-on, and others from overhead. For example, you might feel the character of a wine bottle is best summarised when it is shown in profile, whereas you must step forward and look downwards into a bowl with fruit in it, in order to take in all it represents. Make a painting or collage of your still life.*

You can allow yourself considerable freedom in composing this still life. You need not establish the kind of precise relationships between objects that characterise still life paintings from a fixed position, and you do not have to establish representational three-dimensional perspectival space. However, considerable clarity of thought and rigour is necessary if you are to succeed in establishing a new set of relationships in which overlapping and the distribution of the objects over the whole picture area assume an added significance.

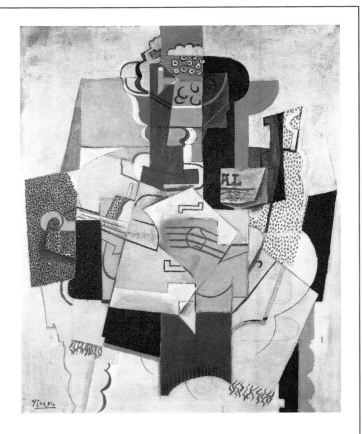

Pablo Picasso, Spanish (1881–1973)
Fruit Dish, Bottle and Violin (1914)
© *Succession Picasso DACS 1998*
Oil on Canvas (92 × 73 cm)

out what angle it is at, and how it relates to the fruit bowl. Picasso said he could paint like Raphael at the age of 14, but spent the rest of his life trying to paint like a child. He also insists he painted what he knew, not what he saw.

What do you think he is trying to tell you in these two statements? Young children also draw what they know rather than what they see. A young child drawing a pram tries to include everything important about a pram – four round wheels, the pram body with a handle, and a baby in it, of course. To represent these as they are, a child shows some sideways-on in profile, and others from overhead in plan view. Can you find any evidence in *Fruit Dish, Bottle and Violin* of Picasso mixing overhead views with frontal ones? Which particular objects are obviously shown as if being seen from above, and which are most clearly represented from a frontal viewpoint?

Hidden Geometry

Abstracted musical forms and shapes provide the basis for the etched designs on the windows of the main entrance doors to the Royal Liverpool Philharmonic Hall. The building has recently been restored to its former glory, revealing these Art Deco windows as an important feature in the concept and design. Among other things, there is the obvious suggestion of a stringed musical instrument in the detail shown. Compare this with the violin in *Fruit Dish, Bottle and Violin*.

Royal Liverpool Philharmonic Hall doors, Liverpool, England Window, Etched Glass

Which of the two do you think was produced first? Think about your initial reaction, and whether you were more conscious of the geometric, abstract aspect of the design, or its musical references of notes, strings and instruments. Does the design successfully convey the feeling of musical harmony through the fusion of geometrical and musical shapes? Do you feel there is a natural fusion of the two, or that one aspect dominates the other?

The Baptism of Christ

We are so accustomed to people specialising in just one aspect of a subject today, it can come as quite a shock to discover that Piero della Francesca, as well as being a great artist, was an equally outstanding mathematician, as well. His profound mathematical knowledge is reflected in his various treatises on geometry, but is not always immediately apparent in his art. Observe how everything in *The Baptism of Christ* is still and poised. This calm mood arouses a tingling sense of excitement, for there is a definite possibility of movement. The three angels will sing, the motionless Holy Dove must flap its wings soon to keep hovering, and the water trickling from the bowl held over Christ's head will wet him in a fraction of a second.

*Piero della Francesca, Italian
(about 1415/20–1492)*
The Baptism of Christ (1450s)
Egg on Poplar (167 × 116 cm)

Even the distinctive square and semi-circular shapes of the painting seem to add to this mood of spiritual calm. On seeing incomplete geometric shapes, many people instinctively mentally complete them. Piero tantalisingly invites you to do so. The outspread wings of the Dove of the Holy Spirit suggest a horizontal line that links with the two short picture edges that jut out beyond the curve of the upper section. There is an obvious similarity between the shape of this dove and the clouds. Do you think it is purely coincidental that one cloud lies on this horizontal line? In completing this line, you also complete the square of the lower section. The Dove hovers above a centrally placed Christ, suggesting a vertical line dividing the painting into two equal halves. St John the Baptist's left arm and the curved form of Christ's loincloth echo the semi-circular top, inviting you to also complete the circle. In doing this, and imagining a horizontal line that touches its base, you discover the distant town that lies along this line, and the two horizontals that divide the painting into three equal sections.

The Golden Section

The Baptism of Christ contains other less obvious geometrical features. If you think of the horizontal line implied by the Holy Dove's wings and the two jutting edges as the base of an inverted equilateral triangle, its other two sides meet on Christ's weight-bearing right foot. This lies on a central axis that is strongly emphasised by the column-like form of Christ's body and the dove. Christ's praying hands cause his upper arms to be angled. The lines they make suggest two sides of an isosceles triangle. They meet on the dove, forming an angle of 36 degrees – the angle of the 'Golden Section'. Whenever this appears in an isosceles triangle, it means the relationship of its base (A) to its sides (B) is on a ratio of A:B as B: (A + B), which can be expressed as follows: 'the shorter part is to the longer part as the longer part is to the whole'.

The Golden Section is a geometrical law of proportion often found in art. Some people maintain that we find it so satisfying because it is present in nature. The size of the leaves on a stem often increase in size as you move down it on this ratio.

It is often used to obtain satisfying proportions in terms of length and breadth in the shape of window frames or pages in a book. In all visual art forms, some artists and designers apply it consciously, others instinctively, because of the pleasing sense of balance and harmony it produces. An obvious way of applying it in landscape painting is in establishing a balance between the amount of sky above the horizon in relation to the landscape below. Is it more likely that Piero, an artist with a knowledge of geometry, deliberately introduced it in *The Baptism of Christ*, or do you think his added awareness simply increased the likelihood of it occurring intuitively in his art?

Practical Activity

Using fairly stiff white paper, cut out a number of geometrical forms of varying shapes and size. Create a composition by arranging these on a grey rectangle, allowing them to touch or overlap where and as appropriate. As well as striving for a pleasing design, try to create a calm, untroubled mood. Restrict the number of pieces, although you may wish to make some large enough to relate to the grey rectangle in ways similar to the circle and inverted equilateral triangle used by Piero on his panel.

As you are using collage shapes, you can keep your design in a constant state of flux for as long as you want without committing yourself to just one arrangement. Treat the activity of constantly rearranging and regrouping them almost as a form of play at the outset. Go on repositioning the various pieces until you sense relationships forming between one shape and another, and the rectangle you are working within. As part of this process, you can periodically introduce new pieces and withdraw others. Treat the negative shapes made by the background as being as important as the white ones, by thinking of the composition as an arrangement of white and grey shapes, as opposed to white on grey.

Once you are satisfied with the composition, make some small studies based on it and experiment with colour or tone. Where one shape is overlapped by another, you can use either colour or tone to suggest the continuation of that shape. You might want to fully complete it, or you may prefer to simply suggest it, as Piero uses the rhythmical form of Christ's loincloth to echo the curve of the semi-circular upper section of the panel, thereby encouraging your eye to complete the circle.

You can introduce colour or tone either by using paint or by replicating certain shapes in different coloured or toned papers. By these means, you can create bold effects, or maintain the restraint and subtlety established by working in white on white and grey. Only when you feel you have taken your experiments as far as you can, and are fully satisfied with the overall effect, do you need to fully commit yourself by finally sticking everything down to make your definitive collage statement.

The Bathers at Asnières

There is also a golden section in *The Bathers at Asnières* by Seurat, another painting already studied in 'Environments' (page 65). The vertical form and silhouetted head of the seated youth divide the painting vertically, forming a rectangle on the right that relates by the same ratio to the larger square area on the left. The youth's pose creates the strongest, most eye-catching vertical division in the composition. There are other less obvious vertical divisions. Which of these do you feel are the more important ones? Vertical lines give a feeling of stability. Do you think the use of vertical lines gives stability to *The Bathers* design?

Seurat had a 'passion for reducing the results of sensation to abstract statements', according to Roger Fry. He maintains that 'gaiety is given by lines ascending from the horizontal, calmness by horizontal lines, and sadness by descending lines'. An obvious horizontal line is formed by the distant bridge, the white wall to its left, and other buildings to the right. Do you feel any others play an important role in this composition, though? He also believes similar sensations are given by tone and colour. Is there a relationship between the horizontal structure and the feeling of calm that permeates *The Bathers*, or do you feel the soft, pastel colours and tones make a greater contribution to this mood of calm?

In addition to verticals and horizontals, diagonals also play an important role in the composition of *The Bathers*. The most obvious is made by the edge of the bank where it meets the water. It moves from the bottom right corner of the canvas to its top left, and is echoed by the form of the man lying on the grass, and the clothes beyond him. Are other diagonals suggested in the way the bathing figures link with the white sail, or the seated youth's clothes with the man in the straw hat? Examine the picture to see if Seurat introduces a less insistent diagonal, moving from the bottom left of the canvas to the top right, as a counterpoint to these. *The Bathers* is a silent, still painting, but do you feel it conveys feelings of sadness or gaiety? Think about whether Seurat's use of diagonals contributes significantly to this sensation.

Georges-Pierre Seurat, French (1859–1891)
Bathers at Asnières (1884)
Oil on Canvas (201 × 300 cm)

Produce a design sheet as the basis for a pair of abstract works of art. Try to ensure that your selective combinations of colour, shape, rhythm, line and brushwork make the mood of each piece unmistakable. Experiment with contrasting ideas by focusing on opposites: harmony and discord; war and peace; order and chaos; calm and disturbance; velocity and sluggishness; restoration and decay; coarseness and elegance, for example. Think about the formal elements you would choose to express the idea of 'harmony', for example. How would you contrast this with its opposite, 'discord'? Considering each theme in the same context as its opposite should help you focus more fully on the key qualities that most vividly characterise each one.

Use your designs as the basis for a companion pair of paintings of similar shape and size, but with totally different in content. Each must express the mood, atmosphere and feeling appropriate to its opposite.

Bear in mind what Leonardo said about the harmonious relationship of one part to another when dealing with 'harmony'. An obvious high priority for any work on this theme is to arrive at a composition that is both balanced and pleasing to the eye, without anything jarring. 'Discord' suggests a much more violent, clashing use of colour and forms. Try to reconcile these requirements with Leonardo's stipulation that your composition should also have formal order, irrespective of its content.

The Martyrdom of Saint Sebastian

On first seeing *The Martyrdom of Saint Sebastian* by Antonio and Piero del Pollaiuolo, your eye is rapidly drawn to the face of the saint. Describe his expression. He is bound to a tree trunk, in an elevated position, and six archers are firing arrows at him. You are obviously attracted to his face out of concern for his plight, but the painting also has an unusually high eye level. It leads your eye upwards, past the archers and the expansive, detailed landscape, to an atmospheric horizon placed surprisingly close to the top of the panel. This horizon is one factor that causes you to focus on his face, set above it against the sky at the very top of the panel. You are equally drawn to his face, though, because of the painting's obvious geometrical structure.

The firmly planted legs of the two outer foreground archers create strong diagonals that rise from the bottom corners, continue through the more distant archers, and finally culminate in St Sebastian and the arrows that already pierce him. These diagonals form two sides of a large triangle. The bottom of the canvas forms the base. Its apex is the saint's head at the centre of the picture, as well as the top. An elliptical shape is formed by the archers' feet, though, and, in conjunction with other equally firm diagonals, these form the base of a three-dimensional cone, or pyramid. Do you 'read' the various diagonals two-dimensionally, or do you feel the painting has a three-dimensional geometrical structure, in keeping with its vast expanse of space?

- *Study the colour scheme. How are colours such as turquoise picked up and repeated? What affect does the olive green of the archer's robe have on the whole landscape, and how does this contrast with the two far archers' robes?*

- *The more fully dressed of the bending archers adds a warm focal point. Where else are similar pinks and reds repeated in the composition? Notice that, central to the whole colour scheme, is the flesh colour that recurs throughout the whole pyramidal form made by the figures. It links martyr and executioners alike.*

- *The colour scheme is clearly carefully calculated. It may have been worked out fully in advance. Is it pleasing, or too contrived for your taste?*

Antonio and Piero del Pollaiuolo, Italian
Antonio (about 1432–98) and Piero (about 1441–before 1496)
The Martyrdom of Saint Sebastian (completed 1475)
Oil on Poplar (291.5 × 202.6 cm)

The Pollaiuolo brothers obviously possessed a considerable knowledge of anatomy. The taut movements of the archers provide the artists with ample scope to portray their muscularity. They achieve this, basically, through just two poses. The four standing archers are all at different angles of the same pose. The two reloading their crossbows also repeat one pose, frontally and from the back. The poses turn and repeat, to create a satisfying rhythmic movement that tightly binds them all together. Do you think this is further helped by an implied circle that passes through the heads of the far archers, the feet of the two central ones, and the drawn-back arms of the outer ones at the panel's edge? Antonio Pollaiuolo was also an accomplished sculptor. Perhaps they might have worked from maquettes. They would have been able to study one pose from a variety of different angles, simply by turning the maquette round to view it from the front, back, either side, and any angle in between.

The Family of Darius before Alexander

Paolo Veronese, Italian (probably 1528–1588)
The Family of Darius before Alexander (1565–70)
Oil on Canvas (236.2 × 474.9 cm)

Like the Pollaiuolo brothers, Veronese used pyramid forms. The bases of the pyramids give a feeling of stability, and their ascending sides draw your eye towards peoples' heads and faces. Allow it to travel from the left hand side of the painting towards the right. The group on the extreme left is bisected by the picture edge, but two spears, one coming in from the left, the other slanting towards it, emphasise their geometrical form. The trailing gowns of the women create a rhythmical sweep into the next group, and this is carried right through to the appealing gesture of the man at its apex. Is your eye immediately pulled back again to the left by the monkey? It curves in that direction, echoing the curve of the man to the right. It acts as a strong counterpoint to him, and this is emphasised by its tonal similarity.

Now follow the line from the apex of the triangle to the bottom right hand corner of the canvas. Look at how Veronese emphasises this line through the rhythms, forms and folds on the drapery of the figures in the main right hand group. Focus on the relationship between the pleading family of Darius and Alexander and his followers. The two groups are physically separated, and you can see through the gap between them. Now you are conscious of the diagonal running from the pediment to the bottom right corner, notice how one geometrical form binds and compositionally links them together.

The Pollaiuolo painting is in oil on poplar. *The Family of Darius before Alexander* by Veronese is in oil on canvas. Do you feel the paint quality differs much in them? The use of oil paint on canvas gained popularity in Venice for many reasons. The salty air and damp humidity of its canals and lagoon were harmful to fresco, there was a flourishing canvas industry for sails, and close trade links with the north, where oil techniques were being pioneered. The panoramic space of the Pollaiuolo is also replaced by the shallow depth of a stage set in the Veronese. You 'read' this painting across its surface, with your eye moving from left to right. Apart from the sky, Veronese restricts you to just one glimpse of what lies beyond the pale coloured architectural backdrop that extends right across the canvas. Through one archway, you see a horse and figure, a receding colonnade, a spire and two silhouetted trees. It is believed the painting was designed to be hung above a tall dado, so its low eye-level would coincide with that of the viewer. This eye-level further emphasises the feeling of sitting in the front row of the stalls at the theatre, looking up at a stage performance.

A dramatic moment is unfolding. Alexander has defeated Darius, the Persian king, in battle. He has sent word that Darius is alive and his family is to be spared. They now kneel before him. The queen has prostrated herself before Alexander's friend, Hephaestion, whom she has mistaken for Alexander. This error is pointed out to her, but Alexander alleviates her embarrassment by saying, 'It is no mistake, for he too is an Alexander'. Veronese places you, the viewer, in the same position as the queen. You can sympathise with her for making such an error, for he makes the two men identical in physique and facial appearance, without telling you which is which. Can you identify them both within the group? Which one do you think is Alexander, and why?

The feeling of watching actors on a stage is further heightened by the row of people on the balustrade of the architecture. As onlookers, they seem to echo and underline your role of looking in from the outside as a spectator. The main protagonists are arranged in groups near the front of the stage. It is almost as if they have been placed there by a director who has carefully worked out in advance how they should be grouped for maximum dramatic impact. Veronese's skilful use of oil paint enables him to capture the textures of pale flesh, white ermine, the silvery and yellowish satins and brocades of the women's dresses, and the way these materials reflect light. The overall impression, though, is that each group stands out as a dark tonal mass against the mellow colour and the paleness of the architecture behind. When you next visit the National Gallery, look carefully at the architectural background. You will be able to see how this contrast has been further exaggerated over time, by fading and increased transparency. Even in reproduction form, observe how the details on the columns have become visible through the two distant horses immediately to the left of the family group.

Colour and Mood

The Umbrellas

Your study of the previous two works will make you immediately conscious of the repetitive curved shapes in *The Umbrellas* by Renoir. The umbrellas' curves become a complete ellipse in the hoop a young girl clasps on the right. Renoir also emphasises the oval shapes of the women's faces and the curving rhythms of the dress worn by the woman on the left and in the bandbox she holds. The curved shape of the girl's arm on the extreme right links with the top of the umbrella held by the woman in the centre, just as Christ's loincloth links with the semi-circular top of Piero's *The Baptism* (page 154). Trace an imaginary circle with your finger through the curve of the girl's bent arm and this umbrella. Does it link sufficiently strongly with anything else to make you suspect Renoir is composing with circular forms in this painting as consciously as Piero, the Pollaiuolo brothers and Veronese use geometrical forms and structures in theirs?

Does the mood of The Umbrellas *indicate a wet winter day or a passing summer shower? Many people have put their umbrellas up, but a partially hidden woman is just opening hers. A tension exists between the angle of her umbrella handle and that of the woman immediately in front of her. They form two sides of a shape that is completed by the open umbrellas above them. You have already observed how de Hooch enjoys creating pictures within pictures (see pages 43–44). When you look at the shape made by these handles and open umbrellas, and the scene it frames, do you feel Renoir, too, is consciously creating a picture within a picture? Focus on this area for a while. Do you find the glimpse of more distant figures and the relationships between them sufficiently interesting?*

Two distinct styles of brushwork are, unusually, used in The Umbrellas. *This is clearly illustrated in the different treatment of the woman on the left and the woman and two children to her right. Try to describe the main characteristics of these two distinct styles. Are they contradictory, creating a lack of harmony and unity in the painting, or do you feel Renoir successfully links one to the other? Another strange feature is that the women wear fashions from different periods. This is because Renoir spent five years on this picture. During this time fashions changed, as did his whole approach to painting following visits to Italy, and to Cézanne in Provence. His great admiration for Veronese is reflected in his earlier soft, fluent brushwork. Following these visits, though, he strove for greater discipline and structure in his art. Which parts do you think were painted prior to his Italian visit, and which after his return? Which clothes are therefore likely to be the more modern, and which show an out-of-date fashion?*

Pierre-Auguste Renoir, French (1841–1919)
The Umbrellas (about 1881–6)
Oil on Canvas (180.3 × 114.9 cm)

An unusual feature of this painting is its predominantly blue colour scheme. Think about whether there is much contrast between the blues used in the earlier, more fluffy kind of painting, and those used for the more dry-looking and severe later additions. For these passages, he uses a modern synthetic colour, French ultramarine, instead of cobalt. To offset all this blue, Renoir introduced complementary warmish colours in the men's clothing and the bandbox over the severely painted woman's arm. Find the details where these complementaries come to their fullest fruition. Do you consider the use of colour in this work to be abstract, rather than naturalistic? Blue is often associated with cold, misery and sadness. We all know what mood someone is in when they are singing the blues! Is this true of *The Umbrellas*, or do you feel its mood is a carefree, happy one that contradicts this notion?

Combing the Hair

In contrast to *The Umbrellas*, a startling array of reds makes *Combing the Hair* by Degas stand out dramatically from whatever else is hung near it. Richard Kendall describes this colour scheme as an amazing 'conspiracy of blood reds and near-oranges, caramels and ash purples', intensified, rather than relieved, by 'drifts of cream and white'. Black lines also show. Some are apparently drawing-out lines, but others – like the eyebrows and mouth of the seated woman – are clearly added later on top of the paint already there. The colour is clearly not 'naturalistic', based on direct observation. Broad brushstrokes, dragged over the surface, allow the coarse, creamy canvas to show through in places. The painting is of a standing woman combing the hair of a seated woman, but it is the abstract nature of the colour scheme and the diagonal rhythmical sweep of the composition that immediately catches the eye.

The canvas of Combing the Hair *is unsigned. Does this and the painting's obvious lack of detail suggest you are probably looking at an unfinished work?*

Perhaps the reds would assume a more conventional place in the colour scheme had Degas continued by adding other colours over the top of them. Details like the creamy patch between the nose and eye of the seated woman illustrate how the painting is building up in dabs and dashes of paint. Do you nevertheless think it strange that such bold, hot colours should be used in the first place to cover the whole canvas if his intention is then to mute them by painting over them? Does the vibrant sensation conveyed by a harmony of piping hot reds appeal to you, though? If Degas had continued, would he have been able to retain the impact of the bold, abstract simplicity of the design, or do you feel there is a risk that the addition of extra details would reduce this?

Hilaire-Germain-Edgar Degas (1834–1917)
Combing the Hair (La Coiffure),
France (about 1896)
Oil on Canvas (114.3 × 146.1 cm)

The Grounds of the Château Noir

A feature of *The Grounds of the Château Noir* is the distinctive patch of pale blue sky. This abstract shape provides the only point of escape from the claustrophobic density of enveloping trees and rocks. Its position in the painting is precisely determined. Allow your eye to follow the main rhythms of the composition. It is led from the bottom right hand corner of the canvas in an upward surge. Observe how the tree on the right ensures it stays within the picture area, whereas the one on the left picks up the upwards movement until it eventually links with a strongly slanting diagonal branch of the right hand tree to 'frame' the patch of sky, making it a focal point in the painting. Does this compositional movement lead your eye in and out of space, or do you think Cézanne uses it to emphasise the two-dimensional surface of his canvas?

Compare the colour scheme Cézanne uses in The Grounds of the Château Noir *with that of* The Umbrellas *by Renoir. Blue saturates them both, but in each case this is offset by small areas of complementary warm colour. The nature of the blues used obviously determines the mood of both paintings. You already know that Renoir added French ultramarine to the cobalt he was already using. This followed his visit to Cézanne, who only used French ultramarine in* The Grounds of the Château Noir. *If* The Umbrellas *was painted in the same range of blues as Cézanne uses, how significantly do you feel this would alter its mood? Conversely, what effect would Renoir's blues have on Cézanne's woodland scene if they were to replace those he prefers? It is apparent that both artists are consciously composing in a range of colour of their own choosing, as opposed to seeking to 'match' their colours with ones they can see in nature. Do you suspect, though, that Cézanne is responding to a scene in which there is a predominance of blues, or do you think it more likely that the powerful mood of this dark woodland area is probably the strongest influence on his choice of colour?*

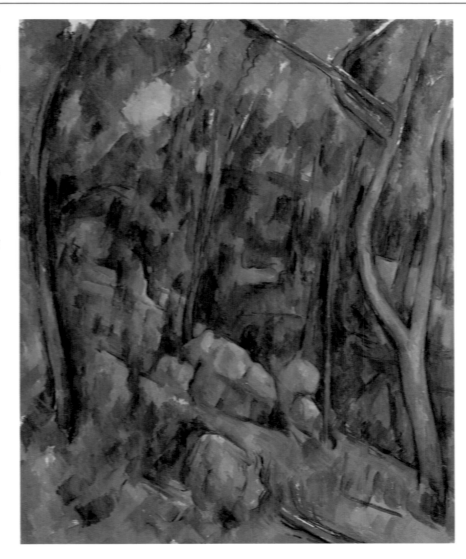

Paul Cézanne, French (1839–1906)
The Grounds of the Château Noir
(about 1900–6)
Oil on Canvas (90.7 × 71.4 cm)

The Côte des Boeufs at L'Hermitage

Make studies of a view of your choice in which the distance is seen through a foreground screen or mesh. This could, for example, be formed by the stems and branches of trees or shrubs, window frames and leads, lace curtain patterns, or the more repetitive shapes made by a wooden trellis or the interwoven mesh of a wire fence. Rather than recording the distance first and then superimposing the foreground on top, reverse the process. Start with the foreground patterns and shapes. Use these to fragment the distance, and then treat this as a series of specific shapes, each worthy of attention in its own right. Focus on each section of distance that is formed by the foreground structure. Record the shapes, colours, tones and textures it consists of. Treat each of these shapes as an abstract arrangement in its own right, without worrying too much about the identity of the objects that form it.

You may find it helpful to take two photographs of your view, one focused on the foreground screen or mesh, the other on the distance. A comparison between the two will help you appreciate qualities within each, and the relationship between them. In choosing your focus, you accept some things will blur and be out-of-focus. The single focus of the camera contrasts with the way artists constantly shift focus as they move from one object to another to represent each in turn. If you have access to a pair of binoculars, also study your view through them, alternating the focus between distance and foreground while doing so. This, too, will help you sense the relationships between near and far, and points of interest within each.

Use all this data to produce a work that emphasises the abstract nature of the forms and shapes contained within each fragment. Is the foreground screen you are looking

through darker in tone than the distance? Does it form silhouette shapes, with the colours and tones of the distance paler but more colourful? The subject is ideally suited to mixed-media approaches and the use of collage, or to the use of impasto effects such as Pissarro achieves. You might also find it constructive to experiment, for example, by establishing the foreground screen using a wax-resist medium, perhaps on fabric. You will then be free to concentrate on the

variety of shapes which make up the fragmented distance. Once the relationship of each to its foreground is established in wax resist, you will be able to focus on its intrinsic abstract qualities, released from the constraint of grappling with the tonal relationships of near and far.

Pissarro clearly emphasises the two-dimensional picture surface of *The Côte des Boeufs at L'Hermitage*. Two people are on a winding path that leads into a scene of farm buildings, hillside and an expanse of blue white sky. It is difficult to take in the various details that make up this view all at once, though. Pissarro makes you look at it through a screen of tall trees and branches that fragment the landscape. In particular, the tree trunks divide the picture into a series of long, thin vertical strips, and you can almost read each of these as a picture in its own right. Which ones do you find the most interesting and satisfying? Each is further broken up by a latticework of branches that constantly criss-crosses it. Look at the points where the view is most obscured by this screen of trunks and branches. Which do you think Pissarro painted first, the distance or the trunks and branches? Study, in particular, the white wall of the farm building. Do you feel it is built up bit by bit, almost as if it was made out of jig-saw pieces, with the shape of each piece determined by the frame of twigs and branches it must fit within?

By working in this way, Pissarro was able to create a strong tension between the surface pattern and texture of the painting, and the space and depth of the landscape itself. Notice how your eye is constantly drawn back to the surface each time you try to focus on the distance where sky and hillside meet. Pissarro increases this effect by deliberately reducing certain objects to their most simple and basic abstract forms. Look at the farm door, for instance. Though you immediately accept it as a door, it is reduced to a simple blue rectangle on a white background. Observe how its size and shape are then repeated in the counter-change of a white rectangle on red made by the chimney stack on the roof immediately above.

The picture surface to which you are constantly invited to return is built up in thickly impasted paint. This richly layered surface was clearly not painted out-of-doors in one go. It has been patiently built up over a considerable period of time. The interlocking textural mesh of the brushstrokes, repeats on a micro scale the bold lattice network of the trees and the fragmented shapes within them. When in the National Gallery, move close enough to this painting to make a careful study of the brushwork. Compare the stippled brushstrokes of the foreground orchard bushes with the feathery twigs and foliage of the trees against the sky, and the white farm walls with the way the clouds are painted. How much repetition and variety can you find in the way Pissarro applies the paint? When close to the painting, the textural maze of brushstrokes seem to assume greater importance than the actual subject matter. Do you find the sensation of simply allowing your eye to roam over this surface pleasurable?

The Water-Lily Pond

The textural mesh of Pissarro's painting is often described as 'woven'. Look closely at the foreground of *'The Water-Lily Pond'* by Monet, and examine the vertical and horizontal brushstrokes. Do these form a warp and weft form of construction that might also be called 'woven'? Think about whether the brushstrokes are random, or whether each 'warp' and 'weft' stroke plays a distinct role in helping to differentiate between the plant life on the surface of the pond and the depth of its reflective areas. Brilliant patches of paint are used to represent the pink water-lily flowers. These interrupt and provide a contrast to the weft-warp effect. Look at the suggestion of depth in the way these light notes of colour diminish in size and intensity the further away they are. In addition to pink, examine the other colours used in the lilies, and look at how they are painted. Is there any evidence of Monet using a combination of vertical and horizontal brushstrokes elsewhere in the painting? Do you feel Monet's brushwork provides textural unity and cohesion in *'The Water-Lily Pond'*?

A Japanese bridge spans the pond. It is seen in such close-up that only its central area is visible. Monet offers you no clues to help you locate it precisely in space. It draws your eye to each side of the canvas, emphasising the picture surface as strongly as Pissarro's line of trees.

The resulting two-dimensional effect is heightened by the absence of sky. The composition is focused entirely on the pond and its surrounding vegetation to an almost claustrophobic degree. Even foliage, rather than sky, is reflected in the small areas of water that show between the water-lilies covering most of its surface. How much extra canvas would be needed at the top and sides to make this a more conventional view with sky and showing how the bridge relates to its surroundings.

Practical Activity

Using a warp/weft structure as a basis, produce an abstract work that emphasises the two-dimensional picture surface and depth. Create the surface effects by using 'weft' marks, and depth by using 'warp' marks. Think of the weft as a melody, and the warp as its harmony. Work in paint, collage or weave, or, alternatively, construct a multi-media work on a section of trellis or by using any other available 'ready-made' grid structure. Establish depth by using warp marks that are restrained in colour and tone.

Study how Monet suggested reflections and the water's depth by this means. Use brighter colours and more vibrant tones and textures in the weft marks to emphasise the picture surface. In addition to depth and surface, you might also experiment with spatial recession by using weft marks of varying size, shape and colour, to suggest varying positions in space. Study the kinds of brushstrokes Monet used to indicate the position of the lilies and foliage in space as well as on the pond's surface.

Compare this painting with Water-Lilies (see page 53), in which sky is reflected. Which of the two paintings, do you think, conveys the greatest feeling of space and depth, and which do you feel emphasises the two-dimensional surface of the canvas most strongly?

In addition to its textural and two-dimensional qualities, do you find you can 'read' the colour scheme and composition of The Water-Lily Pond in an abstract, as well as representational, way? Think about whether Monet chose his colours simply because they were present in nature, or because he was consciously composing in a range of blues and greens heightened with touches of pale pink, crimson and violet, selected expressly to appeal to the senses.

Claude-Oscar Monet, French (1840–1926)
The Water-Lily Pond (1899)
Oil on Canvas (88.3 × 93.1 cm)

Salisbury Cathedral from the Meadows

One of the most awesome geometrical forms in nature is the rainbow. It is difficult not to experience a sense of wonder when you see an unusually bright and clear one. It seems to encompass the whole sky, and links normally separate aspects of the landscape. Apparently, Constable only introduced a rainbow into *Salisbury Cathedral from the Meadows* at a late stage in the planning of the picture. In the midst of the drama of the *chiaroscuro* of a raging storm, the heart of the painting lies in the relationship of this rainbow to the cathedral spire, with the vertical form of the spire providing a central point of order and stability in the composition.

A clearing in the clouds behind the top of the spire creates an effect almost as if a halo is crowning the cathedral. To intensify the impact of the sky, Constable built up the impasto of the clouds with a palette knife. What parts of the painting underline the extent to which its spire provides the focal point of the painting? Allow your eye to roam around the ovoid shape of the features. Are you conscious of a tight tension linking all these various elements together?

John Constable, English (1776–1837)
Salisbury Cathedral from the Meadows
(1831)
Oil on Canvas (151.8 × 189.9 cm)

Landscape with the Marriage of Isaac and Rebekah

Constable was a great admirer of Claude's paintings, and a similar ovoid shape is a distinctive feature of Claude's 'Landscape with the Marriage of Isaac and Rebekah'. It is formed by the dark shapes of silhouetted foliage set against a pale, luminous sky. The larger clump on the right leans towards another, set further back in space. This, in turn, echoes the bending shape, with the link further stressed by a cloud that joins them. Together, they form a kind of canopy that frames the central area of the painting. The role the horses and cart play in Constable's painting is fulfilled here by the wedding groups in the foreground. Though Claude used religious and mythological subject matter in his work, people are usually incidental to the splendours of landscape and light he loved to paint.

Claude Lorraine, called Claude, French (1604/5?–1682)
Landscape with the Marriage of Isaac and Rebekah
(The Mill 1648)
Oil on Canvas (149.2 × 196.9 cm)

The central section Claude frames has tremendous depth to it. Note how your eye is led from the foreground detail of the wedding figures, almost without interruption, to the pale, atmospheric mountain on the far horizon. The shape of this mountain stands out against the lightest area of the sunlit sky. Does this add to the sensation of space and depth in the picture? However, he also encourages you to take a much more leisurely route into the landscape by leading you alternately from one side of the painting to the other, in a slow, languorous way. By this means, he combined depth with breadth.

The massive clump of trees on the right provides a natural starting point. From here, you are led to another clump of trees further in space, to the left. Having momentarily lingered over the tower and building behind them, observe how you are invited to cross the water via the horizontal line of a weir. The landscape behind leads you back across the picture, and the highlighted ruins finally draw your eye to the distant mountain and the vaporous sky.

Saint Jerome in his Study

At first glance, *Saint Jerome in his Study* seems symmetrical in design. However, close scrutiny reveals that whatever is on one side reappears in a slightly different form on the other. Perhaps St Jerome is at work on his Latin translation of the Bible. His raised dais is supported by curved arches on the left and rectangular ones on the right. There is a peacock in the centre foreground. It is facing a copper bowl on the right, but this is balanced by a partridge on the left. A patterned tiled floor leads into the distance to both sides of the dais, but the play of light and shade on it procures distinctly different effects on each side.

A mountainous landscape scene, with figures boating on a river, is quartered by a four-pane window on the left. You also catch a glimpse of it through the windows on the right, but here it is vertically divided by colonnaded architecture that fails to reappear on the left. In front of this, you can make out Saint Jerome's shadowy lion. He was said to have befriended a lion in the desert, and it became his symbol. Above both views are clerestory windows, with a third one in the centre. Even though the composition is severely parallel, there is more sky visible through the right hand one than the left. Even the way light falls on the foreground architecture creates unexpected differences from one side of the painting to the other. Does light enter the picture from the left or the right? Do you think these variations make the painting more interesting than if it was truly symmetrical, with everything on the left exactly the same as on the right?

Claude's smooth paint surface contrasts with the textural brushwork of Constable and the Impressionists. The surface of Saint Jerome in his Study *by Antonello da Messina, is also very smooth.*

Although he worked in Naples, Antonello's paintings reflect the influence of Netherlandish art. Compare the surface quality of this painting with that of van Eyck's double portrait (see page 113). Both are painted on wooden panels, as opposed to canvas. The depth of tone and translucent colour effects made possible by oil paint, enables both artists to achieve a heightened sense of reality.

Do you find the richness of colour, sense of depth and effects of light and shade Antonello achieves convincing? Are you conscious of looking at the saint in his study through the framing device of an architectural foreground? Is Saint Jerome in his Study *yet another example, therefore, of a picture within a picture? It is so close to early Netherlandish art in its qualities that for a time it was even attributed to van Eyck.*

Antonello da Messina, Italian (active 1456, died 1479)
Saint Jerome in his Study (about 1475)
Oil on lime (45.7 × 36.2 cm)

Make a series of studies of symmetrical architectural facades. Look for any variations in design or detailing that distinguish one side from the other. Does the way light and shade falls on the facade create any differences in how the two sides appear? A window on the left might form a dark shape, for example, but the corresponding one on the right catch the light to form a reflective surface. Ravages of time, restoration work or subsequent modifications might also create variations between the two sides. Where these exist, do they make the building appear assymmetrical, or do they give added variety by creating a play between symmetry and balance in its design?

Working in any medium or combination of media, use this information to produce an abstract work in which there is a tension between symmetry and balance. Achieve this by establishing variations in the shapes, textures, tones and colours of one side compared with the other that are subtle enough to maintain a feeling of symmetry, yet are pronounced enough to create a balanced design because of the way in which they echo or complement each other.

Minerva protects Pax from Mars

Peter Paul Rubens, Flemish (1577–1640)
Minerva protects Pax from Mars
('Peace and War', 1629–30)
Oil on Canvas (203.5 × 298 cm)

The god of war, Mars, raises his shield to protect himself from Minerva, who lunges at him to chase him away. Does the swivelling movement of Mars' attendant Fury suggest he is about to flee?

His neutral colour and rhythmic movements merge with those of the sky. Notice that everything in this section seems to flow into everything else, but in an uncomfortable way. The dark turbulence of 'War' contrasts strongly with the clarity of light and geometrical order of 'Peace'.

The incidents representing 'War' are not as immediately clear. Is this because they occur behind those to do with 'Peace', or because they take place in a murky, shadowy light that makes them indistinct? Do you sense any relationship between foreground and background in the way Mars' black armour and shield echo the circular shape of the leopard and cornucopia, though?

Think about whether Rubens deliberately emphasises this contrast between the darkness and chaos of war, and the harmony, order and prosperity of peace.

The first impression on seeing Rubens's *Minerva protects Pax from Mars* ('*Peace and War*') is of dynamic, turbulent movement. A strong diagonal from top left to bottom right divides the canvas into two triangular halves.

The foreground incidents, all relating to 'Peace', fit mainly within the lower triangle, and those to do with 'War' in the upper one. Look at how these two areas are affected by the play of light and shade. Everything to do with peace seems to revolve around the circular shape formed by a tame leopard, rolling on its back like a playful cat, and a cascading cornucopia full of luscious, juicy fruit. The satyr on the left, and Cupid, the god of Love, and Hymen, the god of Marriage, leading children to the cornucopia from the right, increase the sense of circular movement in space. Behind, Peace squirts milk from her left breast to feed the small child Plutus, who clambers towards her. The pale flesh colour of Peace causes her to stand out against the dark tones that surround her. Her head is at the apex of the kind of triangular shape with which you are now familiar. Like other examples you have seen, its base is the bottom of the canvas, and its sides spring from opposite corners.

Rubens was a successful diplomat as well as an artist, and in 1630 he presented this painting to Charles I (see page 70), while in England as an envoy for Philip IV of Spain. The purpose of his mission was to bring about peace between Spain and England. On the successful conclusion of such a mission, it is easy to understand why, as a gift, he should choose to offer the king a picture that so powerfully contrasts the benefits of peace with the destructiveness of war.

Practical Activity

Using collage and mixed media, make an abstract work of art that combines order with chaos, structure with flux. Develop your ideas using sketches and photographs of details that exist within your locality. Focus on made structures with a clearly defined form and order which are in the process of being reclaimed by nature, or are subject to vandalism.

Decay and erosion or attack by fungus and lichens might introduce irregular and organic forms on what was once a purely rigid and geometric structure.

Introduce tone and colour, selectively, as Rubens does, to create a counterpoint and contrast between the areas that represent order, form and structure, and those to do with irregularity, chaos and flux.

Bacchus and Ariadne

The glorious array of colours revealed when Titian's *Bacchus and Ariadne* was cleaned and its yellow varnish removed in 1969, are so intense you feel drawn towards it every time you see it in the National Gallery. Richness of colour characterises other Venetian paintings in the same room, but here it is so intense it would stand out in any company. It is both sensuous and skilfully organised. The blues are at their richest in Ariadne's robe, and are further intensified by the contrast with her vivid red sash. In spite of the abundance of blues, the colour has great warmth, with even the sky assuming a warmer hue in a broad central band above Bacchus' head. Other aspects of the design are equally rich and complex. It is a fitting painting with which to conclude a chapter on the Abstract, for they all have a role to play in the expressive and visual representation of a famous mythological story.

Bacchus, the god of wine, leaps from his chariot towards Ariadne as she searches for her lover, Theseus. He has abandoned her, and is sailing away aboard a ship you can see on the horizon to her left. Bacchus is returning from India, accompanied by a strange assortment of revellers. A young faun trails a calf's head behind him, and a half-naked woman, who echoes Ariadne's pose, is clashing symbols. A satyr brandishes an animal's leg in one hand, Ophiuchus is entwined by a serpent, and the drunken Silenus is slumped on a donkey.

Tiziano Vecellio, called Titian (active about 1506, died 1576)
Bacchus and Ariadne, Italy (1522–3)
Oil (identified) on Canvas (175.2 × 190.5 cm)

Many of the design principles already considered in this chapter can be found within this one work. As in the Rubens, a strong diagonal divides the canvas, but this one runs from top right to bottom left. It contributes to the strong rushing movement that threatens to carry your eye straight out of the canvas. This is emphatically stopped, though, by the firmly planted pose of Ariadne on the extreme left, affirmed by the circular constellation of stars above her, and a white fleck in the cloud just below them. As well as stopping the movement, this strong vertical also keeps your eye within the composition.

Further vertical and horizontal divisions are suggested by the relationships between clouds, tree trunks, the pose of Bacchus, the horizon line, and the way peoples' heads and limbs relate to one another. Are there enough to make you suspect the painting might even have an underlying grid structure? Which items play a key role in the overall design and structure of this composition?

Even though Ariadne is still reeling from her lover's rejection, Bacchus requests her hand in marriage. He offers her the sky as a wedding gift. To her eternal glory, she will become a constellation of stars within it! You can clearly make out their circular form, above her head, close to the top of the canvas.

Bacchus' billowing cloak is particularly eye-catching. Observe how it lies on a diagonal that runs from the top right hand corner of the composition directly to Ariadne. The angle of his head and left leg, however, lie on a counter-diagonal that leads to the constellation of stars from the opposite corner. Compare how Bacchus and his followers fit into the triangular shape on the right made by these two diagonals, with the way Rubens also groups the incidents relating to Peace within a triangular shape in his gift to Charles I.

Titian sets all this drama and activity within an expansive landscape. Allow your eye to linger for a few moments on the delicate flora at the bottom right hand corner of the canvas, and then move inwards, past the two static cheetahs, and into the distance. Are you conscious of the meandering nature of this journey as you follow the line of the cliff top, take in patches of sunlight, clusters of buildings, and then the atmospheric, distant mountains? Having arrived at the horizon, it is natural to travel along it. This brings you to the ship. It is easy to overlook this, but it is crucial to the story. Do you feel the way Titian finally leads you to it actually adds to its impact? You immediately realise that Ariadne's twisting pose describes her reaction to it, with Theseus aboard, as it is expressive of her surprise at the leaping Bacchus.

Universal Themes Within One Painting

Many of the works you have studied within the context of one chapter, are equally worthy of consideration within another, of course. Piero's *The Baptism* and Seurat's *Bathers at Asnières* both appear in this chapter and Environments, but their treatment of the Human Figure is also noteworthy and *The Baptism* is a significant event. *Bacchus and Ariadne* could easily feature in all six chapters. You have already considered the **abstract** qualities of its colour scheme and compositional design. Do you feel the painting possesses harmonious relationships of the kind Leonardo believes to be the most satisfying aspect of a painting? A worthwhile way to conclude this book is to briefly highlight how each of the other five themes manifest themselves in Titian's *Bacchus and Ariadne*.

The painting positively teems with **human life**, activity and energy. It vividly illustrates the kinds of psychological and formal relationships that connect people who are caught up in a powerful human drama. Titian obviously has the necessary ability to portray them in a wide variety of postures and movements, for he clearly possessed a sound anatomical knowledge of the human body.

He demonstrates this through a wide range and variety of twisting poses, actions and gestures that enable him to bring everyone vividly to life within the context of a powerful human drama.

This drama is set within a spacious **environment** beneath an expansive sky. Titian is able to lead you into the depth of the landscape through his understanding of atmospheric perspective. Every glimpse he provides of distant buildings, the sea below the cliffs, and the fields above seems truthful. The whole scene is bathed in an early morning light, with flickers of sunlight breaking through a cloudy sky that promises a fine day without the threat of rain.

Every detail of the plant life and vegetation is consistent and convincing. Your eye can linger on the detailed representation of the foreground **flora**. A domesticated black dog with white paws and a red collar provides a counterpoint to the more exotic, but equally convincing cheetahs, with their black spots and tufts of white fur on their bellies. The tall, luxuriant trees are splendid in their own right and play an important role in the design of the composition.

The painting dramatically describes an important **event**, the encounter between its two main characters. Bacchus leaps from his chariot to propose to Ariadne. Her surprise at his arrival and reaction to his promises at a time when she is still feeling the loss of the departing Theseus is vividly portrayed in her twisting pose. The whole scene is full of revelry and action. It leaves you in little doubt that something important is taking place and that Titian is a compelling storyteller.

You are conscious that every detail is significant to the drama, and that if you devote sufficient time to this painting, each one adds an extra layer of meaning.

The painting tells a mythological story, and is full of mythological characters that highlight its **fantastic and strange** aspects. Towards the back of the group of figures following Bacchus, the drunken Silenus, his head garlanded, sits astride a donkey. A dancing satyr, part man and part goat, waves an animal leg in the air. A smaller satyr struts happily along in the foreground, while behind him a bearded, tanned figure, inspired by the recently discovered classical sculpture of Laocoon being strangled by sea snakes, struggles to free himself from the serpent wrapped round him.

Bibliography

I hope some of the questions posed in *Understanding and Investigating Art* will arouse sufficient curiosity in students to make them want to find out more from other art books. The titles listed below are particularly helpful, and most justify shelf space in any school Art & Design library.

The National Gallery Complete Illustrated Catalogue
Compiled by Christopher Baker and Tom Henry.
National Gallery Publications, London, 1995.
(Also available on CD-ROM.)

Every work in the Collection is succinctly described and illustrated, and a thumbnail sketch of each artist is provided.

Art in the Making: Impressionism
David Bomford, Jo Kirby, John Leighton, Ashok Roy.
National Gallery Publications, London in association with Yale University Press, 1990.

Written in support of an exhibition, this book contains fascinating information about the techniques and working methods of the Impressionists. It is well illustrated and includes X-rays of paintings, photographs showing layers of paint, and impasto using raking light.

Perspective and other drawing systems
Fred Dubery and John Willats
The Herbert Press Limited, London, 1972.

Making and Meaning: Turner The Fighting Temeraire
Judy Egerton
National Gallery Publications, London, 1995.

Written for an exhibition about the painting, it contains important new material.

Seurat
Foreword by Anthony Blunt
Encyclopaedia Britannica International Limited, 1971.

Large colour plate format, but also contains an influential essay on the artist by Roger Fry.

Africa Adorned
Angela Fisher
Collins Harvill, London, 1984.

This magnificently illustrated book deals with every aspect of personal adornment found in the many art forms practised throughout Africa.

100 Great Paintings: Duccio to Picasso
Dillian Gordon
National Gallery Publications, London, 1981.

Follows the popular format of text on one page opposite the picture in question.

Making and Meaning: The Wilton Diptych
Dillian Gordon
National Gallery Publications, London, 1993.

> *Written to coincide with an exhibition about this painting, it includes some fascinating details from the Diptych in the plates.*

Hall's Dictionary of Subjects & Symbols of Art
Introduction by Kenneth Clark
John Murray, London, 1974.

Hall's Illustrated Dictionary of Symbols in Eastern and Western Art
John Murray, London, 1994.

> *Both the titles are an invaluable aid to working out symbolic significance and meaning in paintings and sculptures.*

From the Land of the Totem Poles
Aldona Jonaitis
The American Museum of Natural History, New York, 1988.

> *Provides many insights into the lifestyle, customs and art of the American Northwest Coast Indians, best known in this country because of their carved totem poles.*

Degas: Beyond Impressionism
Richard Kendall
National Gallery Publications, London, 1996.

> *Doubling as an exhibition catalogue and a book, this magnificently illustrated tome provides numerous interesting insights into the artist, and his life, work and working methods.*

The National Gallery Companion Guide
Erika Langmuir
National Gallery Publications, London, 1994.

> *Deals with over 200 paintings in the National Gallery. Contains relevant information about the works themselves, places them in their historical and artistic contexts, and provides information about the artists who painted them. A measure of its worth is that, at key moments in my writing, I invariably found within it whatever information I required.*

The Penguin Dictionary of Art & Artists
Peter and Linda Murray
Penguin Books Limited, 1978.

> *A quick and useful guide to basic factual information about a wide range of topics.*

An Introduction to Auckland Museum
Stuart Park
Auckland Institute and Museum, 1986.

> *A noteworthy Maori section includes interesting plates and information about the canoes.*

Art
Auguste Rodin
Hodder & Stoughton, London, 1912.

> *Fascinating insights into an artist's mind based on conversations with a friend.*

Looking at Indian Art of the Northwest Coast
Hilary Stewart
Douglas & McIntyre Ltd, Vancouver, 1979.

The text and clearly-drawn diagrams deal with the forms, cultural background and structures of this highly imaginative art in the context of the peoples' myths and legends.

The Collections of the British Museum
Sir David M. Wilson
The Trustees of the British Museum, 1989.

Provides an invaluable overall picture of the British Museum collections, including the works normally housed in the Museum of Mankind. Students might find a lack of information about some of the works illustrated frustrating on occasions.

Myths and Legends: Paintings in the National Gallery
Felicity Woolf
National Gallery Publications, London, 1988.

A great deal of fascinating detail is packed into this slim book. It proved extremely useful during the writing of the 'Fantastic and Strange' chapter.

Kaffe Fassett at the V & A: Knitting and Needlepoint
Kaffe Fassett
Century Hutchinson Ltd, 1988.

Art and the Built Environment
Eileen Adams and Colin Wood
Longman, 1982.

Selections from the Notebooks of Leonardo da Vinci
Irma A. Richter
Oxford University Press, 1977.

Tops of the postcard pops
L. Marks (Based on an interview with Neil MacGregor, Director of the National Gallery, London)
The Observer, 27.12.1992.

List of plates

Index